A Faithful Man

Equipped to lead as prophet, priest, protector and provider

J. Mark Fox

Antioch Community Church
1600 Power Line Road
Elon, NC 27244

(336) 586-0997

markfox@antiochchurch.cc

www.antiochchurch.cc

◆◆◆

"Most husbands and fathers have a desire to lead their families, but they testify that they don't know how to lead. Mark Fox has solved that problem in his book *A Faithful Man*. Flowing out of a passion for Jesus Christ to be glorified in the lives and families of those who bear His name, Mark provides clear, biblical, practical, doable encouragement for men as leaders of their families. The heart-warming personal stories, interesting illustrations, and helpful examples make the book relational as well as entertaining. As you read you feel like you're visiting with a friend, a fellow-laborer in the field of family life. *A Faithful Man*, written in a simple, easy-to-read style, invites you to read on attentively much like someone prospecting for gold stays at his task – the prospect of another treasure on the next page or in the next chapter. Any man who seriously desires to be a Christ-like leader of his family will be encouraged and equipped by Mark Fox's *A Faithful Man*."

—NORM WAKEFIELD, Author, Speaker, and Executive Director and Founder of The Spirit of Elijah Ministries International, Bulverde, TX

"J. Mark Fox has provided the men of the contemporary church with an insightful handbook on what it means to be a Christian father. Grounded in Scripture and theologically sound, Fox writes in such a way that allows any man, wherever he is in his Christian walk, to understand, act upon, and fulfill his God-given right and responsibility to his family. This is a necessary book for the Christian home both today and in the years to come. What is so refreshing about the manner in which Fox writes is that he is not afraid to admit and confess that he has had to learn much of what he writes about through trial and error. Even more refreshing is the fact that he readily acknowledges he is still learning. Mark Fox demonstrates through his excellent illustrations, his brilliant use of Scripture, and his own personal testimony that men are called and directed by God to live a lifestyle of discipleship within their families."

—W. RYAN STEENBURG, Ph.D., Associate Pastor of the Christian Home, First Baptist Church of Prospect, KY; Executive Director, The Council for the Family-Integrated Church; Founder and Director, Daddy Discipleship

"J. Mark Fox has provided a simple, profound and very readable instruction manual for men. If the men of our culture can capture the character represented in Mark's four "P's", our homes will be strengthened, our churches will be strengthened, our economics will be strengthened, our culture will be strengthened. Thank you, Mark, for offering such powerful help in such an easy pill to swallow."

—MARK HOLDEN, husband, father, teaching elder, conference speaker, business man from Finger Lakes, New York.

"Mark Fox has done it once again! In his entertaining, easy-to-read style, combining profound spiritual insights with immensely practical examples and ideas, Mark has successfully tackled the crucial topic of men becoming the spiritual leaders of their homes. Every man *can* and *should* read this book!"

—BRAD SHEDD, Associate Pastor responsible for the Household Worship Service at Harvest Assembly in Chesapeake, VA. He and his wife, Alyson, have been married for 21 years and have eight children.

"*A Faithful Man* is so readable! Never becoming bogged down in complicated doctrinal schemes, the reader emerges from this book with a delicious entree of sound doctrine and a savory side of practical application. Without condemning the audience, Mark Fox leads the way – making us want to follow. He offers warm encouragement, packed with real-life illustrations-stories with which we can all identify. I read this book in two sittings, and loved every page. Though not a how-to book, if we take it to heart, we will know how to be better husbands and fathers. Every man-father, elder or Christian leader-will profit from this book, which should make us all more *equipped to lead*."

—ERIC BURD, President of Household of Faith Fellowship of Churches in Portland, OR; an Elder in his local church, Vancouver Household of Faith, Vancouver, WA. He and his wife, Jerry, have been married for thirty-seven years and have five children.

"*A Faithful Man* contains the perfect blend of Biblical truth and personal experience to challenge and exhort men to godly leadership. J. Mark Fox humbly explains what wives wish husbands knew and gives fatherly advice that children want their dads to hear. You will be inspired and challenged by these heart-warming stories and Scriptural directives."

—TONY ROSE, Assistant Director of Information Systems and Technology at Elon University, married twenty years to Audrey, the father of two daughters, a spiritual mentor and friend.

"The reader of *A Faithful Man* will not find the words of some armchair theoretician, but rather the solid counsel of a man who, by God's grace, has and is leading his family well. With sound biblical exegesis, relevant illustrations and warm personal stories, Mark Fox sounds a heartfelt call for men of God to be genuine followers of Jesus as well as faithful disciplers of their families. May the Lord bless you with grace to both understand and practice these principles for His glory and your family's good."

—WADE COX, D.Min, Pastor of Nall Memorial Baptist Church, Graham, NC, and Adjunct Professor of Theology, Liberty University Online, Lynchburg, VA

"Being a godly husband and father is a great, high calling. I deeply appreciated Mark's stories, encouragements and Biblical challenges to rise to this calling by God's grace. This book is full of extremely practical instruction and action steps. Mark's straightforward, down-to-earth style is refreshing. *A Faithful Man* is an excellent resource and a must for your personal or church library."

—JOE DENNER, Pastor, Dover Bible Church, Dover, IL, and President, Alliant Leadership

"The introduction to *A Faithful Man,* recounting Fox's relationship with his own father, captured me and convinced me to read this book! Mark Fox lives and writes this encouraging challenge for men who desire to grow in their leadership. Addressing their indispensable roles as prophet, priest, protector and provider, Fox applies solid Biblical perspective. If our churches and homes are to have maximum multigenerational spiritual growth, maturing men must lead the charge. I am using this valuable tool to equip men in my own church.

—CRAIG BOWEN, husband, father and pastor, Lakeside Community Church, Middleburg, FL

A Faithful Man

Equipped to lead as prophet, priest, protector and provider

This book is dedicated to all of the faithful men in my life who have modeled manhood for me, helped me grow up, and taught me how to love, live, and lead for the glory of God! I am particularly grateful for my brothers at Antioch Community Church who live these truths out every day.

I am grateful for Lisa Pennington, Jon Gregory, Chrissy Hahn, Daniel Sigmon, Tony Rose, and my wife and most trusted editor, Cindy, for all of their proofreading and editorial help.

Table of Contents

Introduction xvii

1. You Cannot NOT be the Head 29

2. They Changed Me. 35

3. Sweet, Sweet Song of Salvation 45

4. Teach Your Children Well. 53

5. God Must Love Normal Guys. 64

6. Passion Communicates 69

7. Proclaiming His Praises to My Family 79

8. Worship On! 95

9. Keeping It Real 107

10. Are You Not a Man!? 116

11. Building the Hedge 125

12. Touching Their Hearts. 131

13. Improving Your Vision. 139

14. Holding Their Hearts. 153

15. Numbering Our Days. 167

Conclusion. 175

Appendix A: Small Groups for Accountability. 179

Appendix B: Four Testimonies of Family Devotions. . .183

A Faithful Man

Introduction

When I was a little boy, I believed like most little boys that there was nothing my dad could not do. He was a tall man, 6' 3", and had grown up as one of eight children. He had neatly combed blond hair that was always perfectly in place. His blue eyes and his bronze tan made Dad handsome, and he always looked younger than his years. He loved it when people raised their eyebrows upon finding out his age or that he had a son who was old enough to graduate from college. "You're not that old, Ed!" they would exclaim. "There's no way you are forty." He would grin and wink at us, smiling like he had just won the Masters or something. Growing up in a big family, being lost in the shuffle much of the time, had left Dad insecure in some ways. He regretted that he had not been able to go to college and spoke often about his desire to see his three boys make up for that in our own studies. He was fragile, it seems to me, in some ways. But life's hard knocks had also made him capable, self-reliant, extremely proud of his ability to do anything he put his mind to. He always fixed the lawn mower or the car himself. I remember seeing Dad lying on the floor in the laundry room while Mom held a flashlight as he replaced the belt on the washer. He loved the yard and took great pride in keeping the grass neatly manicured and the bushes trimmed. He always had the best garden in the neighborhood and spent hours in the summer, after work in the evenings and much of the day on Saturday, tending to it. He loved to watch things grow, and we talked about his green thumb. Though I never got excited about the garden or fixing the car or anything else that was broken, I was proud of the fact that my father could do those things.

I loved to hear Dad tell stories about his childhood. He told us what it was like growing up the son of a mechanic, with not enough love or money to go around. He told us how he picked up acorns in the yard for his Aunt Claudia, who paid him something like five cents a bushel. He told us about his father lining him and his brothers up and taking his belt off to give them a spanking. I recall the account of how he and his friends were up to no good one night, and in their attempt to escape getting caught, they were fleeing through someone's back yard when Dad was clothes-lined. Literally. He hit a clothesline going full speed and was very fortunate not to break his foolish neck. I remember sitting at the table with Dad and some of his siblings and listening to them pick on each other, telling stories about how they grew up and pranks they had played on each other. I loved it. I guess that's one of the reasons why I love to hear and tell a good story, and it's why I also love to write. I got that from Dad as well.

I also inherited a love for sports from Dad. He told us a thousand times about his prowess on the mound as he pitched for his high school baseball team. He was a southpaw, and he made sure I knew how important left-ies are to the success of a team, to the point I almost felt cheated I was born a righty. He was the one who taught me to throw and catch a baseball, and we spent hours in the backyard when I was little, Dad patiently teaching me proper form. The first year I played baseball, I had to try out. Even though I was eight years old, I had to run out on the field when they called my name, and in front of all the teams' coaches, I fielded grounders and pop flies and then came in to bat. On the way home that day, Dad told me that when it was my turn to try out, the coaches called, "Next: Jimmy Foxx." Dad loved that, because Foxx had been a star in the Major Leagues in the 30s and 40s when Dad was a boy. I didn't have a clue. All I heard was "Fox," and took off running as fast as my stubby little legs would carry me, scared to death but wanting so badly to make Dad proud.

Dad talked about his basketball career, too, and showed off his old-style hook shot whenever I was playing basketball with my brothers or a friend. I would shake my head and laugh, but Dad would keep shooting at the goal until he got his timing back, and then he could hit one hook shot after another. I learned to love watching basketball on TV because that's what Dad and Mom did. As much as I liked Bob Verga and the Duke basketball teams he played on, I fell in love with Carolina Blue as a young teen. Coach Dean Smith, Charlie Scott, Larry Miller, and Dick Grubar were household names at the Fox's, and I tried my best to dribble and shoot like those guys. Whenever we watched North Carolina play, I would sit with my notebook and record every point that was scored for each team. I prided myself on always knowing the score, and Dad would ask me during timeouts and commercials, since they didn't always show the score on the screen like they do now. I never let him down; I was on it. Dad was always thorough in everything he did, and I guess I learned that if you are going to do something that is important to you, then do it right. His garden was weed free. His cars ran like tops. His carpets were spotless. His hair was perfect.

The trouble started when I reached puberty. That's about the time I discovered how much I longed for Dad to tell me he was proud of me and to ruffle my hair, give me a little punch on the arm, or a slap on the rear. I remember we had this little routine, my brothers and I. We would be told to go to bed, and we knew what that meant: go upstairs, put your pajamas on, brush your teeth, and then come back down to say goodnight. We would run up the steps, get it done and run back down, and while standing in the doorway of the family room, we would say, "Good night, Mom and Dad. See you in the morning. Love you." Dad would not look up from his paper, but he would respond with, "Good night." Mom would look up, give us a big smile and say "Good night," and then she would always say, "I love you, too, boys." At that, Dad would say,

"Love you, too." I didn't think anything about it at the time. It was normal to me, and that's the way I figured it was in every house.

I thought all kids said, "Goodnightmom'ndadseeyou'nthemornin'loveya." And all dads kept reading or watching TV while saying good night, and all moms smiled and said, "I love you." If I beat my brothers downstairs, then I got an "I love you" from Mom that I didn't have to share with the other two. This was about the same time of *The Smothers Brothers* comedy show, and I could relate to the banter back and forth between Tommy and Dick Smothers about which one of them their Mom loved the best. I suspected that Mom loved me the best, but I didn't say that to my brothers. I also didn't say to them that I didn't really *know* whether or not Dad loved me. As I said, I didn't think about that when I was little, not that I recall. It was when I reached 12 or 13 and my body started to change and my hormones started raging and I started wanting to resist or reject my Dad's authority that I began to look at Dad with a more critical eye. I wanted something from him then, and didn't really know what it was. All I could see was that he seemed to care more about his car and his house and his hair than he cared about me. When I was 15 or so, I rewrote Don McLean's "American Pie" song that was all the rage in the early 70s. In my version, my fantasy was that I drove Dad's prize Buick to the levee (you know, the one that was dry in the original song?), and shoved it over the edge. "Bye, Bye, Electra 225..."

I remember sharing that song with my older brother and he laughed himself silly, which gave me satisfaction. Still, my heart was yearning for a dad who would care for me like he did his car and his golf clubs. I wanted to hear Dad ask me about me, but it seemed that even if he did ask me a question, it was only a way to turn the conversation back to himself. "How was baseball practice today?" he would ask. I would start to answer with what we did that day, and he would seem half-interested for a moment and then launch into a speech about his career, his fearsome fast ball, his popularity in high school, his hopes for a career in the Major Leagues...

When I complained to Mom about this as a high schooler and later as a college student, Mom would nod and sympathize. "Your dad really does love you," she would say. "He just has a hard time showing it. But he's proud of you and your accomplishments in school and in sports. He tells other people about it all the time."

That was the line I heard my whole life. "He is very proud of you. He brags about you with his buddies on the golf course all the time." That was nice to hear, but it didn't scratch my itch. It didn't satisfy my deep longing for my dad to look me in the eye, shake my hand, and say, "I am proud of you, Mark. You are a good man and I love you."

~~~~~

My guess is that all of you men reading this book grew up wanting from your own father the same thing I did. And most of you didn't get it. What does a man do if he grew up like I did? Where does he find his manhood? How does he grow past what may be a deficit in his soul from being raised by a father who did not affirm his son? These are the questions I want to answer in this book.

I realize that many people reading this will shake their heads as they growl, "You had a father who *lived* in the same house with you? What are you complaining about?" Or, "You had a father who didn't come home drunk every night? Or who didn't beat you to a bloody pulp once a week, just for fun? Or who was married to your mother and not fooling around on the side with half the women in the neighborhood? *What* is your problem?!"

I understand.

Compared to many, I had it made. But is that really the issue? If God has ordained in His Word that a father is to bring up his sons and daughters "in the training and admonition of the Lord," (Ephesians 6:4), then *that* is the standard. If a father's job is to *exhort and comfort and charge* every one of his children, as Paul wrote in 1 Thessalonians 2:11, then *that* is the standard. When God's standard is violated, no matter how much or how little, there will be consequences in the lives of those who violate that standard and in the lives of those who are under the authority of those who violate that standard.

I have met many men over the years who are struggling with their manhood or who are abdicating their responsibility to lead in their family, some who are clueless about how to love and disciple their children, others who are failing in the most basic of disciplines.

Paul says in 1 Corinthians 11:3, "But I want you to know that the head of every man is Christ, the head of woman is man, and the head of Christ is God." I would like to spend some time unpacking how I understand this verse works itself out in the life of the man who says to God, "OK, I see it clearly stated in Scripture that I am the head of my household. But I don't know what that means. I don't know how to do it. I don't even know if I *can* do it." Then he adds one more very important statement and an even more important question: "God, I *want* to know what it means, and I *want* to obey You, and I *want* to lead my family, and I *want* to learn how to build godly relationships with my family—but I am so afraid I will fail. Will You help me?"

That's what this book is about. I want to help men discover the truth of 1 Corinthians 11:3. I believe understanding our role as leader in our homes is key not only to revival in our homes, but to revival in our churches, and even to revival in our nation. Richard Baxter, the great Puritan pastor and writer, said, "You are not likely to see any general reformation until you see family reformation."

There is a deeper truth, too, that I pray will be fruit from this work. That truth is that you and I will know our acceptance and love from our heavenly Father, and that knowledge will transform our fatherhood, making us free to love Him and those whom He has entrusted to us. Milton Vincent writes in his powerful little book, *A Gospel Primer*, "Outside of heaven, the power of God in its highest density is found inside the gospel. This must be so, for the Bible twice describes the gospel as 'the power of God.' Nothing else in all of Scripture is ever described in this way, except for the Person of Jesus Christ. Such a description indicates that the gospel is not only powerful, but that it is the ultimate entity in which God's power resides and does its greatest work." (pp. 14-15)

What a wonderful promise we have, men, for it is the power of the gospel that makes us able to perform all that we have been called to do by God. What a powerful truth that the gospel changes us so that we *can* be the faithful man God made us to be, which brings glory to Him!

Are you with me?

Chapter 1
You Cannot NOT Be the Head

A friend of mine, Marc Jantomaso, stated in a workshop with pastors, "It's God's heart to train men." He compared the kingdom of God to a mountain and drew a picture on the whiteboard. "See, the base of the mountain must be large and broad enough to support the rest," he pointed out. "If the top of the mountain is broader, more developed than the base, the mountain will topple over. The base consists of mature believers, disciples, and disciple-makers who are invested in the lives of younger, less mature believers. The kingdom of God is expanded as the base is expanded. If we add souls but the base is not expanded, souls will fall off the side!" Marc went on to explain that one of the ways we can build the base is to equip and train men to lead, and especially to help men understand and walk in their responsibilities as the heads of their households.

Paul wrote in 1 Corinthians 11:3, "But I want you to *know* that the head of every man is Christ, the head of woman *is* man, and the head of Christ *is* God. (emphasis added)" Which part of this verse do we have the hardest time "knowing" in a way that demonstrates obedience and victory? I don't think there is much serious debate about Christ being our head, or about God being Christ's head. It is the second clause that gives us fits and has been misunderstood by the church today. The head of woman is man. Seems simple enough, and it really is. As Douglas Wilson emphasized in *Reforming Marriage*, this is not a command but a statement, a fact: every man *is* the head of his household (pp. 22-23). It is an indicative, not an imperative. God does not command man to be the head of woman; He simply states the fact, the reality, the truth of His design. Man is the head of woman. As some have said, you can be a bonehead, a meathead, a musclehead, an airhead, or a knucklehead...but you cannot *not* be the head. So, why not do whatever it takes to be a godly head?

There are some reading this book who could say, "I know what that means and I am doing it faithfully, by God's grace." I praise God for you brothers who are leading your families faithfully and seeing the fruit of your labor. There are others reading this book who could say, "I think I know what that means, but I know I am not leading my family in a consistent manner." I praise God for you brothers as well, for your willingness to admit that, like *all* of us, you need some encouragement and some instruction in these things. There are still others reading this book who could say, "I don't have a clue what you are talking about. I love my family, but I don't know what it means to be the head. I am not really the spiritual leader in my home, but I want to be. I just don't know where to begin." I praise God for you brothers, as well, for your honesty. The only place God can really deal with us is where we really are. As I heard years ago, you have to be real with God if you are going to be right with God.

Consider another analogy with me. What do you have to do when you realize that you have traveled 100 miles in the polar opposite direction of your intended destination, and instead of being 100 miles closer to the beach with your family, you are 100 miles closer to the mountains? You have to admit your mistake, which will include turning around...going the other way. That's repentance, and it is the very first step toward getting there. If you are not willing to admit you are going in the wrong direction, well, have a great time in the mountains! Let me know how all those sand toys and boogie boards work out for you in the woods. Here's the thing, though: the only one you will be fooling as you sit under the tall pines in a beach chair, wearing your bathing suit and flippers and holding your shell bucket—will be you. Your family will not be fooled, or even slightly amused. Neither are they amused in the least with a father who claims to be headed in the right direction in his leadership and is as far off the beam as he could possibly be. Get real.

Paul said, "For if anyone thinks himself to be something, when he is nothing, he deceives himself. But let each one examine his own work, and then he will have rejoicing in himself alone, and not in another" (Gal. 6:3-4).

Dad took my two brothers and me to Sears once when we were little, and this clown-head helium balloon machine in the store captivated my younger brother. Eric begged Dad to give him a balloon until my father relented. Dad put a quarter in, pushed a lever, and a balloon popped out. Now, he was supposed to put the balloon firmly on the nozzle that came out of the clown's mouth, then push the red button that was his nose so helium would rush into the balloon. The problem was that Eric got so excited when he saw the balloon pop out he pushed the clown's nose, and the helium started rushing out of the nozzle before the balloon was in place. Dad frantically tried to get the balloon on there in time, but could not do it and clearly lost his cool in the process. The balloon ended up pitifully small and still earthbound. It dragged behind my younger brother, who was crying, while Dad fumed, frustrated that his efforts to do something to please his son ended in tears.

That scene has been played out in my own fathering many times. I have tried to lead my sons or teach them or please them, only to be frustrated at the results or at my own selfishness when my efforts failed to please. As I have asked the Lord to help me be a better father over the years, He has graciously taught me and led me and helped me to repent again and again.

The next few chapters outline a man's responsibilities as the head of his household in four ways: as prophet, priest, protector and provider. You will not find these four terms used to describe a husband in the Bible, but the principles are there. I first heard these four roles mentioned at a conference, wrote them down, began to chew on the idea, and decided to search the Scriptures for biblical understanding. It was John Calvin, writing in his classic work, *Institutes of the Christian Religion*, who said, "the office which [Christ] received from the Father consists of three parts. For he was appointed . . . Prophet, King and Priest." (Book 2, Chapter XV:1, pp. 425-426). If Christ is head of the church as our prophet, king, and priest, then I believe it is the father who is called by God to stand before his family, in Christ, and fulfill the same roles: "But I want you to know that the head of every man is Christ, the head of woman is man, and the head of Christ is God." (1 Corinthians 11:3) For the function of king, I substitute protector and provider, for a couple of reasons. First, it may be more palatable for a society that is decidedly *not* a monarchy to avoid referring to men as kings. The term may carry unwanted baggage. Second, the primary leadership responsibilities of the kings of Israel were to protect their people as the head of the army, and to provide for their people as the head of the state.

Let's begin with an examination of the role of the family prophet.

Part One: Faithful Men as Prophets

Chapter 2
They Changed Me

A prophet is, above all, a teacher, a person who speaks truth into another's life and makes a difference.

I had lots of teachers growing up. I remember Mrs. Miller, my first grade teacher, with great fondness. She was white-headed and a tiny woman, at least in my memory. She was soft-spoken and kind, but Mrs. Miller was also not afraid to discipline her young pups when we got out of line. I can still see her face after she popped me on the back of my hand with a ruler. As I gazed up at her, red-handed and surprised, she said, "Mark, that was just a little love tap." I don't think at the time I was convinced about whether it was just a tap, but I was certainly convinced of her sincerity to teach me and the rest of us without distraction, though there were interruptions in that first grade classroom that had nothing to do with my misbehavior. November 22, 1963 stands out in my memory like it was yesterday. I can still see the brown box speaker that hung on the classroom wall, and I can hear Mr. Dyer, the principal, informing the whole school with sadness that our president, John F. Kennedy, had been shot. Mrs. Miller was our counselor that day.

I have not forgotten Mrs. Beck in the sixth grade. I was going through puberty, or it was going through me, and I could be a pain in the rear end whenever I chose to be. A dodge ball game stands out in my memory. We were outside in the grass beside Old Town Elementary School, standing in a big circle like you do for dodge ball. Mrs. Beck was standing off to the side watching us. The ball was thrown to me, and I glanced over and saw that Mrs. Beck was distracted by something else, and her back was turned. So I flung the ball at her as hard as I could. It hit her squarely in the head. She turned back, face flushed, eyes flashing, angry and disappointed, and...crying. I felt really bad that I had done it, but in order to save face in front of the other boys in the class, I just started laughing. I told you, I could be a real pain. She could have had me kicked out of school, but she chose not to. She pulled me aside and asked me why I did it. Looking into the face of a teacher that I genuinely liked, I just shook my head and lost the tough guy attitude and said, "I don't know, Mrs.

Beck. I really don't." If Mrs. Beck taught me something that day, it was forgiveness.

In the 11th grade, Mr. Goodwin was the Key Club advisor, my English teacher, and the man in charge of the concession stand at the football games. Mostly, he was the first one to really challenge me with learning vocabulary words and improving my writing. Every Monday we would get ten new college-level words in his class, and every Friday we would have a test on those ten words plus all the words we had already learned. That's where I learned words like vicissitudes and triskaidekaphobia. Useful words? Not so much. But I thought it was so cool to learn big words like these, and I took the challenge seriously. Compared to how much I worked (or, how little) for my math and science classes, I learned those words like it was my *job.*

I remember Mr. Goodwin for something else that year. I decided during the fall semester that I really didn't want to go to school five days a week. I mean, are you kidding me? Five days in a row? What were those people thinking? I decided that I could keep up and do just fine if I went only four days a week. So, I started skipping. It was easy since both of my parents worked and had to leave the house every morning before I did. When my ride came to pick me up, usually friends of mine from the neighborhood who had their own cars, I would just stick my head out the door, hold my head or my throat like I was deathly ill, and wave them on. Then I spent the morning doing challenging and intellectual things like watching TV game shows. I would catch up with Monty on *Let's Make a Deal*, laugh along with a much younger Betty White on *Password* and try my shopping skills with Bob Barker on *The Price is Right*. The rest of the day, I would just sleep or read a book or wander around the house.

Then it happened. My dad just happened to run into Mr. Goodwin at a local meeting of some kind, and my English teacher said, "I sure hope everything works out with Mark. I have been really concerned about him."

"Huh?" Dad responded. "What do you mean?"

"Oh, well, with Mark being so sick this semester and missing so many days, I figured he must really have some serious health issues," Mr. Goodwin said.

My goose was officially cooked. My dad assured Mr. Goodwin that the only health issues I had were about to be inflicted on me when he got home. I can see Mr. Goodwin's face in my mind right now; he had this little mischievous grin, accented by a sly wink, when he was teasing one of his students about something. He said one day in class, "Boy, it sure is a good thing Edison invented the light bulb. Do you know why, Sturdivant?" He aimed his question at one of the football players in our class who was not known for his mental agility.

"No, sir. Why's that?" Sturdivant responded.

"Because if he hadn't invented the light bulb, we would all have to watch TV by candlelight," Goodwin said with a perfectly straight face.

Sturdivant screwed up his mouth, scratched his head, and said, "Uh, yeah, I guess you're right, Mr. G." Then he continued to work on that dilemma in his brain while "Mr. G" gave the rest of the class his trademark grin and wink.

I never had the courage to ask Mr. Goodwin if he was wise to me all along, if he figured out I was just skipping all of those days that semester. But I think I know.

When my Dad got home from his meeting that night, he called me into the family room where he and Mom were waiting for me. He told me the story he had heard from Mr. Goodwin, and asked me to tell him what I was doing all those days I was at home instead of at school. Then he said, "You have a choice to make, and you're going to make it tonight. You will either go to school every day for the rest of your high school career, or you will pack your bags and move out of this house and go find another place to live. The only way I will subsidize your lifestyle with free room and board is if you agree to live by MY rules. And my rule is that you go to school every day."

I didn't have to think long about that decision. That's how I lived to graduate with my class of 632 in 1975.

If Mr. Goodwin taught me something besides vocabulary words, it was honesty. I had lied to him, my parents, my friends, and my other teachers that whole semester, and Mr. Goodwin found a way to force me out of hiding. I am grateful for that. I don't know what would have happened to me otherwise.

Those were the schoolteachers who shaped my childhood and teenage years in some way. But there were others in my life in those days that I remember because they taught me about God.

Pastor Ted Key, my first preacher, was the one who came to my house and explained to me what it meant to become a Christian. I had told my parents I wanted to do that when I found out, at eight years old, that in order to get the juice and the crackers when we had communion, you had to be a Christian. So, my parents asked the pastor, and he came over and told me how to become one. He was a nice man, but I honestly don't remember anything about that day or even the Sunday after when I walked down the aisle at the end of the service and announced to the church that I wanted to get saved. I was baptized at the next baptism service, but I don't remember anything about that either, just that the water was cold and deep, especially for a little squirt like me.

I don't remember anything about my spiritual development between the time I walked the aisle at eight and the time I went on a retreat with the youth at fifteen. Nothing. I played a lot of Little League baseball during those years, and went to church and Sunday School and Royal Ambassadors every week. I went on vacations to the beach every summer with my family and my mom's parents. I grew up...a little. But I don't remember learning to study the Bible, or to pray, or to hear God's voice, or to tell others about Jesus. Perhaps I was hearing all of that at church, but I wasn't hearing it at home. This is why dads are key, at least in my opinion. More on that later...

When I was fifteen years old, I decided that I would go with the church youth group for a week at Ridgecrest

Baptist Assembly, nestled in the Blue Ridge Mountains of North Carolina. The week started off with the bus ride, and all of us who were headed up the mountain for just a joy ride were sitting in the back. I had taken up smoking, so when Norma fired up a cigarette on the way up, she and I enjoyed it together. I shake my head, even now, when I think about how brazen we were. I also wonder like some of you readers: Where were the chaperones? I cannot tell you, but for whatever reason, we were left to our own devices for the three-hour trip to Ridgecrest.

Up on the mountaintop, things went downhill pretty fast. In between skipping sessions to walk around and look for chicks, as the guys and I called it, we also hatched up a scheme to get some beer. Now, I had never *had* a beer, mind you. But when one of the older teens suggested we make a beer run and asked who was in, I shot my hand up.

I don't remember the details of how it all was supposed to go down. I just know we got caught. Before I could say, "Help me, Jesus," we were ushered into a room in the cabin, one at a time, to meet with Pastor Holland. I was scared spitless, and when it was my time, I thought I would pass out just walking through the door and into this man's presence. Don't get me wrong; I liked Pastor Holland. He lived up the road from me and had two sons, one of whom was a few years younger than I. Pastor Holland had been in business for a while before being called by God to seminary and to pastor, and I admired him for being willing to make the sacrifice to do that. A simple man who loved the outdoors, especially his garden, he also enjoyed a great sense of humor, and was a good preacher who always had interesting stories and illustrations in his sermons. Now God was going to use him as a hammer, and I was a piece of steel on His anvil. The truth is, I don't remember a word he said to me that day. All I know is that God spoke through that pastor to a young rebel, and my life was never the same again.

I had been caught by the pastor, but more importantly, I had been apprehended by the Lord. Isn't that what happened with Jonah when he was trying to run away from God's call on his life? He was caught by the big fish, but he was apprehended by God. David was caught by Nathan the prophet, but he was apprehended by God. Peter was caught by the young maiden's questions before a charcoal fire, but he was apprehended by God. In each of these men's lives, a turnaround took place. Their moment of greatest shame was the beginning point for their greatest ministry. As Stephen Olford said, "God often has to crush a man before He crowns him; He breaks a man before He blesses him." God certainly broke me that week. In fact, I believe that was the week when I became a Christian, where the Lord gave me faith to believe Him and follow Him. I wanted nothing more than to be His disciple. I had heard Luke 9:23 my whole life, but that week it meant something to me: "If anyone desires to come after Me, let him deny himself, and take up his cross daily, and follow Me." That week, I really prayed to Him for the first time, and for the first time in memory had the outrageous thought , "He's really there! And He really does love me." A relationship with my Savior had begun.

Chapter 3
Sweet, Sweet Song of Salvation

The bus ride down the mountain after that week at Ridgecrest was wildly different for me and a few others in the group. We had been to the mountaintop, and we had seen the hand of God. I determined, along with four other young people on that bus, that when we got back home, we would begin to tell other people about what Jesus Christ had done in our lives. That's where Hugh Greene came into focus.

Until the week of my salvation at Ridgecrest, I really didn't pay much attention to Hugh and his ministry. He had youth meetings, and I had been to some of them, but Mark was the center of his own universe. I was the sun, and the world revolved around me. This was my world; everybody else just paid rent, as the saying goes. But not after Ridgecrest. I came down from the mountain after my Copernican Revolution, with a new understanding that Jesus Christ is the Son, and my life revolves around

Him. I went back to the youth meetings with a new spirit...literally. I told Hugh that what had happened to some of us at Ridgecrest was too good to keep to ourselves. "We need to tell everybody we know," I said.

I didn't know about the four lepers starving to death outside the Samarian gate in 2 Kings 7, but we were in the same situation. Those guys were going to die. The city was under siege by the Syrians, who were camped outside the city and slowly starving the Samarians to death. The four lepers looked at each other one day and said, "Why are we sitting here? If we sit here, we die. If we go into the city, we die. Why don't we go surrender to the Syrians? What is the worst thing that could happen to us? Oh, yeah, we could die. But, we might not!" So, they traipsed off to the Syrian's encampment. Meanwhile, God had caused the Syrian soldiers to hear something that wasn't there, the presence of chariots and a huge army, and they had all fled from camp, leaving everything they owned behind. The four lepers stumbled into the deserted camp bug-eyed, not believing their good fortune, going from tent to tent eating, gathering silver and gold, eating some more, scavenging, eating, until they suddenly stopped, gravy dripping off their chins. They said, "We are not doing right. This day is a day of good news, and we remain silent. If we wait until morning light, some punishment will come upon us. Now therefore, let us go and tell the king's household." (2 Kings 7:3-9)

That's the way I felt after my conversion: though I deserved death, I had stumbled onto life that I had never dreamed even existed. I know now that God did it all, just like He did for those four lepers. He led me to Ridgecrest, He apprehended me there by grace through faith, and He brought me down to the valley with a vision for reaching others. I could not keep this to myself. Oh, no. "Evangelism is like one beggar telling another beggar where he found some bread." Except I didn't find it. God found me. And it wasn't just bread; it was the Bread of everlasting Life. And I was not a beggar; I wasn't even interested in the things of God when He met me on the mountaintop and won my heart.

Five of us met with Hugh Greene, and we told him that we wanted to start inviting our friends to come to the youth meeting on Monday night, but there was a twist. First, we said, we want to actually go to their houses and sing some songs and give them our testimony. He was a bit skeptical of how well this was going to work, but he said to go for it and sent us off with his blessing. That next day was a Monday, so we started talking to our friends about what had happened to us at Ridgecrest. And we lined up our first prospect for Monday night visitation. We showed up at his doorstep at around 6:30 or so, five of us with two guitars. He nervously invited us into his living room, and we plopped down on the chairs and sofas and began our planned presentation. It was very simple. "Bob," we would say, "We went to summer camp last week at Ridgecrest in the mountains, and something very exciting happened there."

"Really? Uh, what was that?"

"Bob," we would say, "we met Jesus."

Then we would sing a few songs we had learned at camp. One was written by Larry Norman, and it was called, *Sweet, Sweet Song of Salvation.* It was a catchy little tune and included some clapping and some "nah, nahs," and the chorus went as follows:

Sing that sweet, sweet song of salvation
And let your laughter fill the air
Sing that sweet, sweet song of salvation
Tell all the people everywhere.

Sing that sweet song of salvation

To every land and every nation

Sing that sweet, sweet song of salvation

And let the people know that Jesus cares.

We would get into that song, sing it at the top of our lungs. And we loved the words of the first verse:

When you know a pretty story

You don't let it go unsaid

You tell it to your children

Before you tuck 'em into bed.

And if you know a wonderful secret

Well, you gotta' tell it to all of your friends

You tell 'em that a lifetime filled with Jesus

Is like a street that never ends.

"Bob, we know a wonderful secret, and we just had to come and tell it to one of our friends." One of us would share our testimony of how Jesus Christ had saved us, and how our lives were changed because of His sacrifice for us on the cross. Then we would sing another song, possibly an old James Taylor favorite:

When you're down and troubled

And you need a helping hand

And nothing, whoa nothing is going right.

Close your eyes and think of me

And soon I will be there

To brighten up even your darkest nights.

You just call out my name,

And you know wherever I am

I'll come running, running, yeah

To see you again.

Winter, spring, summer, or fall,

All you have to do is call

And I'll be there, yeah, yeah, yeah.

You've got a friend.

We would sing it loud and soulfully, just like James did, only not quite so nasally, and then we would end our visit with, "Bob, there's no friend like Jesus. All of your other friends, ourselves included, will come running to help you when we can, but we can only come some of the time, and we can only help with some of your problems. Only Jesus can come and help anytime. Only Jesus can solve all of your problems. Only Jesus can save you from your sins.

Would you be interested in learning more about Jesus with us? Because we are going back to the church now to meet with the youth pastor and study the Bible together, and we would love for you to come with us."

More often than not, "Bob" answered yes. And for the record, we only went to Bob's house once.

By the next summer, that group of five teenagers had grown to more than fifty. Revival was taking place at our church, and not just with the youth. Many of the teens who started coming to church and were born again began to invite their parents and their siblings to come. Some of the parents had faithfully dropped their teens off at church for months before they started coming on Sunday themselves. I remember that one of the young men we had invited to church in those days, named Mike, became a Christian. He started in on his father to become one, too, and his father saw the transformation that only Christ can do as He worked in his son. It wasn't long before Mike's father was led to Christ by the pastor, Burke Holland.

I grew a lot over the next three years before heading off to college. God had graciously put men in my life who took time to encourage and teach me. He had started getting my character ready for the seed of His Word as a child, under the leadership of people like Mrs. Miller, Mrs. Beck, and Mr. Goodwin. Then when the fullness of time had come, God sent forth His Son into my heart, and used people like Pastor Burke Holland and Hugh Greene to teach me about Himself. They were prophets to me and others, and God used them to shape my character and point my life.

This is what fathers are called to do for their own children, to shape their character and point their lives, to fit them like arrows for the target for which God has created them. Let's talk about this job description for dads.

Chapter 4
Teach Your Children Well

What was a prophet? The word can be found throughout the Bible and can mean many things. But if we take it down to its barest essentials, I believe we can agree that a prophet has four big items on his to-do list. The first two are essential, and the third and fourth, which we will address in Chapter 6, cannot be accomplished without them.

First, a prophet is someone who has heard from God; God has spoken His Word to him and revealed His truth to him. Second, a prophet is someone who communicates what he has heard from God to others, specifically, to the people of God. A prophet who hears from God but does not speak for God is like a stagnant pond. Water comes in, but none goes out, and, as a result, nothing can live there. A prophet who speaks for God but has not heard from God is like a polluted pond. Something foreign in the water has poisoned it, so that nothing can live there. A prophet who hears from God and speaks what he hears is a healthy pond, brimming with life and watering the landscape all around. Better yet, he is like an artesian well. In fact, the Hebrew word for prophet, *nabiy*, comes from a root word that means, "to cause to bubble up, to pour forth." The prophet bubbles up and pours forth the words of God, which, like a spring, nourish and give life and refreshment to all who hear.

The key to this life-giving ministry is a vital relationship with the Lord Himself. Jesus said it like this, "He who believes in Me, as the Scripture has said, out of his heart will flow rivers of living water" (John 7:38). If you aren't privately seeking the Lord in His Word and through prayer, your heart won't be tuned to hear from Him.

OK, so I know what some of you are thinking as you read this. "It sounds like he is talking about pastors and preachers and Bible teachers. Those guys are the ones who bubble forth the Word of God. Not me! I am just a dad."

That would be fine except for one very large elephant in the room that we just cannot ignore. Don't look. He is standing right beside you, and he is *huge!* And he is looking right at you with those big, soulful elephant eyes that say, "Look at me. Listen to me. This is important." The elephant in the room is the Truth of God's Word, and it just simply cannot and must not be ignored. Here is what the Bible says in Ephesians 6:4, "And *you, fathers,* do not provoke your children to wrath, but bring them up in the training and admonition of the Lord" (emphasis added). The first three chapters of Ephesians clearly portray the position of the Christian, and the last three chapters clearly picture the practice of the Christian. Paul only gives one word of instruction specifically to the fathers, the verse quoted above. First, the negative, here is what you don't do, Dads. "Do not provoke your children to wrath." (More about that later.) Second, the positive, here is what you must do, Dads: "Bring your children up in the training and admonition of the Lord."

"Bring them up" is from a Greek word that is used only twice in the New Testament, once in Ephesians 6:4 (above) and in Ephesians 5:29. "For no one ever hated his own flesh, but nourishes and cherishes it, just as the Lord does the church." It is interesting that both times this word is used, men are addressed, as husbands in Ephesians 5 and as fathers in Ephesians 6. In each case, the admonition to the man is to act towards another, for whom he has responsibility, in a way that provokes growth and blessing and maturity. He is to nourish his wife as he nourishes his own flesh. He is to nourish his children, also, bringing them up to maturity and wisdom. The other time this word is used in the Scriptures in reference to training or educating can be found in the Septuagint, the Greek translation of the Old Testament, in Proverbs 23:24. "The father of the righteous will greatly rejoice, and he who begets a wise child will delight in him." Don't be confused by the word "beget" and think that a wise child will just emerge from your wishful thinking. Slap yourself, Dad, you're dreaming. The father of wise children rejoices to see the fruit of his labor, as he has been intentional about bringing them up in the training and admonition of the Lord.

This combination of training (in this chapter) and admonition (in Chapter 5) is the one-two punch of correction and instruction. Think about it. When your child was one year old (or even younger), you mainly trained by correction. "No," you would say as he reached for the hot iron or began to make his way to the fireplace. You would stop him from carrying out his will by pulling his hand away before he burned himself. It was more correction than instruction. It involved discipline, and of course, training your little one to obey. That sounds like

Paul knew what he was talking about when his first word to children in Ephesians is, "Children, obey your parents in the Lord, for this is right" (Ephesians 6:1). It is our job as parents, and specifically Dad's job as the head of his household, to train his children to obey the Lord by obeying their parents. If we have not taught our children to obey our commands, we will not be able to bring them up in the training and admonition of the Lord.

Cindy and I have always taught our children that obedience involves three things, if it is to be biblical obedience. First, we have taught them to obey immediately. The child who has been taught to wait until his mom explodes before he obeys has been trained in delayed obedience. This could prove to be deadly. Donald Grey Barnhouse used to tell the story about a missionary serving overseas in a place where highly venomous snakes lived. The missionary father looked outside one morning to see his four-year-old son squatting in the dirt, playing with his toy truck. Dangling in the tree limb just above his head was a deadly viper. The father walked to the doorway of the house and called his son's name quietly. The boy looked up at his father who said, "Drop down and begin to crawl to me, Son." The boy obeyed immediately. "Now get up and run to me!" the father cried, and the son ran into his father's arms. His father held him and turned his face around to see the snake hanging just above where his head had been a moment before.

Imagine that the four-year-old was the typical product of a household where permissiveness is the watch-word of the day. He had never been forced to do anything he didn't want to do. He had learned how to get out of any distasteful chore and how to stay up as long as he wanted. He had been trained by his parents that he really didn't have to obey until they began to count. "Johnny, I am going to count to five, and then you're going to get it if you don't let little sister out of that head-lock...one...I mean it, Johnny...two...you're really going to get it!. . . three... don't make me go to five, Johnny...four...I mean it, Buster, you're in BIG trouble if I get to five....I mean it, Johnny, let your sister go!. . . Don't make me say five, Johnny..." Meanwhile, little sister's face has turned beet red and is changing to purple.

What would have happened to little Johnny on the snake-infested mission field? Well, I think you know. Obedience? I think not. I heard a college student say a few years ago that she turned down a nanny job with a rich family, even though the job included a huge salary, a car to drive, use of the family pool, and trips with them to exotic places. The student she was telling this to asked why in the world she turned such an offer down. She replied, "Because the lady said, 'I have one rule that you must never violate if you are going to be my child's nanny. You may never ever tell her no.'" What happened to that little girl growing up in the lap of luxury, having no one with the backbone to correct her, discipline her, teach her obedience? I don't know, but she may have been better off with vipers.

The second quality of biblical obedience is that it is done joyfully. You remember the story of the little boy in the back seat of the car who would not sit down and would not put on his seatbelt. His mother told him over and over to do it, and he ignored her. When she'd had enough, finally, she reached back and pulled him down by his belt, slammed his rear on the seat, and demanded with veins popping all over, "Now, put your seatbelt on!" The little tyrant snapped the buckle together and glared at his mother in the rearview mirror. She looked at him and said, "Well, you're sitting down *now*, aren't you?" To which the little rebel replied with a smirk, "I'm sitting on the outside...but on the inside, I am *standing*!" If the little boy had obeyed the very first time his mother spoke, but did so with a scowl on his face and a grumble in his heart, that would have been defiance as well.

Finally, biblical obedience is complete obedience. I remember the silly commercial of the car wash place that charged you five dollars to wash your car...but they didn't rinse it. "We never said we would *rinse* your car, sir," the attendant said to the hapless man with the soapy sedan. Partial obedience is disobedience; we can all think of times when our children obeyed part of what we said, but improvised the rest. As a result, the meal was ruined, the tools were lost or rusted, the room was a train wreck, the car's engine was melted. OK, maybe that last one was Dad's fault!

When our son Judah was three, he liked to pretend he was Davy Crockett or Daniel Boone. He would dress up in his buckskins, don his coonskin cap, take 'ole Betsy and his powder horn, and head off into the backyard to trap and shoot wild animals. Since we lived in downtown Graham at the time, and our backyard consisted of a little bit of grass, a small garden, a swing-set and a few trees, Judah had to use his imagination. The wildest animal we ever encountered in our yard was a family of possums who decided to take up residence under our back deck. So, Judah mainly shot at invisible mountain lions and imaginary bears. That was hard work, though, and after a while, a frontiersman out in the wild works up a powerful appetite, so Judah Crockett would come in for supper. The problem was, the grub was not always what a pioneer like Judah was expecting.

"Broccoli? Davy Crockett doesn't eat broccoli!" Judah said when he spied the unholy vegetable on his plate.

"He does if he wants to hunt mountain lions," his mother replied. "Broccoli gives pioneers energy and strength, and besides, you have to eat it. If you don't, you will have it for breakfast in the morning. And I don't think Davy Crockett ever ate broccoli for breakfast. Yuck!"

Judah Crockett was caught on the horns of a dilemma. "Do I eat the broccoli now, so I can hunt lions and bears in the morning after a good breakfast of eggs or cereal?" He pondered that option. "Or do I refuse to eat it and hope that Mom will forget about it in the morning?"

Judah refused the broccoli, and was told that he would see it again in the morning. He slept fitfully that night, dreaming he was Davy Crockett being attacked by a giant broccoli tree that kept trying to eat him up. But when he woke up, the sun was shining, the lions and bears were out there waiting to be trapped or shot, and Judah hit the floor with a smile, excited about life on the frontier. When he got to the chow hall, drawn by the smell of cooked pork, he saw the rest of the family sitting down to a scrumptious breakfast of eggs, bacon, and toast, and then the dream he had all night became a nightmare. His plate was there, and all that was on it was last night's broccoli.

"Where's my breakfast?" Judah asked, knowing the answer but hoping maybe that this was all a cruel joke.

"Right there," his mother replied. I added, "Judah, you were told last night what the deal was. If you want to be able to go outside and play this morning, you are going to have to eat your broccoli."

Judah slumped in his seat, his chin on his chest, his hands hanging at his sides, defeated on the outside, but stubborn as the wildcats he hunted on the inside. "I won't do it," he thought. "I will not eat my broccoli. Yuck!"

The lions and the bears had the run of our backyard that day because Judah Crockett's will remained strong until late afternoon. He finally gave in, and learned two valuable lessons. First, he was the child, we were the parents, and he would have to obey. Period. Second, he learned that "no chastening seems to be joyful for the present...nevertheless, afterward it yields the peaceable fruit of righteousness to those who have been trained by it" (Hebrews 12:11).

Back to Ephesians 6:4, then. The first job of a prophet is to train his children to obey Dad and Mom...immediately, joyfully, completely. Now you are ready to add understanding and wisdom to that obedience by teaching your children the Word.

Chapter 5
God Must Love Normal Guys

O K, we talked about correction in Chapter 4. This chapter is where instruction comes in.

Men, we are to be the ones who, more than anyone else, teach God's Word to our families. Think about it. I get one hour a week as a pastor to teach God's Word to the people of Antioch Community Church. The dads in the church get the other 167. The problem is, the typical dad in the typical congregation is not using any of those 167 hours to train up godly children. Why not?

Here's the key: he must be convicted that it is his job. Ephesians 6:4 says, "And you, fathers, do not provoke your children to wrath, but bring them up in the training and admonition of the Lord." The Word commands us to do it. But the Word commands us to do a lot of things that we don't do, or we start doing and then stop. If it is a conviction that you must bring your children up in the training and admonition of the Lord, that you are the prophet of your house, responsible for hearing from God through His Word and prayer, and communicating with the rest of the family what He is teaching you, then family devotions are essential. You will be able to start and maintain family devotions if this is your conviction. But it must be a conviction. What if it's not, and you want it to be? Pray. Repent. Ask a brother to pray for you. If conducting family devotions is a preference, then anything that comes along can bump it off your radar. If it is a conviction, then national disaster or personal tragedy may delay you, but nothing can stop you. So, get started on doing what is right, and pray for the conviction to come in God's time.

Second, you need to have a plan for family devotions. If this is something new for you, I would recommend that you *keep it very simple* to begin with. Meet for fifteen minutes, and the best way to do that is to pick a fifteen-minute slot during the day that is going to be the most consistent. For us, that happens to be first thing in the morning. For some, it may be at bedtime or at suppertime. But if you pick suppertime, that may eliminate three out of seven nights if you are not home together every night for supper. If so, you have limited your impact as prophet. Maximize the time. Once you have a time, choose a plan. We have used many different things for family devotions, and I can make suggestions for you. But here's the bottom line: you need to read Scripture together. Pick a book of the Bible you want to take the family through, Dads, and then read a chapter every day. Proverbs is a great one. Take turns reading. I do the math real quick and divide up the verses among the members in my family. Right now there are six of us at home, and everybody reads. It seems like yesterday that there were nine at home, but only four or five could read. Divide up the verses, and read the chapter. Next, go around the circle, asking each child to share something they learned from the text, or to ask a question about something they didn't understand. This has been one of the most exciting and challenging things about family devotions for me as a father, because my children can ask some very tough questions. Encouraging them to ask questions has forced me to study more, to dig deeper, to cry out to the Lord for wisdom in His Word.

After your time in the Bible, spend some time praying. I will usually ask for prayer requests. Then we get on our knees to pray, partly because that posture discourages sleep, and partly because a physical attitude of weakness and dependence helps promote a spiritual humility in prayer. We go around the circle, and each one has to pray, even if it is just a sentence. They also need to pray out loud, and in a voice that everyone can hear. I have told my children that the only reason we have some of the great prayers recorded in the Bible, like the one the disciples prayed in Acts 4, is because someone wrote them down after hearing them. There is a time for us to pray silently, but this is not that time.

Here's the really exciting news. Leading family devotions as the prophet in your house does not require a Bible or seminary degree. You do not have to be an elder in your church, or even sing in the choir! As Gregg Harris likes to say about the church, "It runs on regular." Same with family devotions. They run on regular. Normal guys can do it, and as they say, God must really love normal guys like you and me, because He made so *many* of us!

Here's more exciting news: twenty-one days a habit makes. That means that if you start tomorrow morning and do this Monday through Friday, you will be *hooked*, totally addicted, in less than a month. It may take that long for your children to get used to getting up a little earlier, too, so be patient. Don't be upset with yawns and grumbling. Expect resistance at first, possibly even from your wife. A friend of mine wanted to have family devotions, but was having trouble getting buy-in from his wife, mainly because she was used to sleeping a little later, and this was going to change the schedule for her. Finally, he said, "Honey, wouldn't you like to be able to look back twelve months from now and say, 'We had family devotions consistently for a whole year?'" She admitted that she did want to be able to say that. "Well, then," he said, "can I hold you accountable for that by waking you up for family devotions every morning?" She agreed, and now they have been consistent for several years, and it has been a blessing to their family.

Though family devotions are a non-negotiable and the very cornerstone of your home discipleship, there is much more you can do to teach your children the Word. Make it a topic of conversation at the dinner table. Bring up something you heard on the radio, or at work, and ask, "What does the Bible say about that?" Read good Christian biographies aloud after dinner. Discuss movies you watch as a family and the worldview that is presented and how it lines up with or conflicts with Scripture. In other words, talk about the Word as you sit, as you walk along the way, as you lie down, as you *live* together as a family. (See Deuteronomy 6.)

Chapter 6
Passion Communicates

We have seen so far that a prophet must hear something from God which he then communicates with his family. What are the third and fourth things a prophet must do?

He is a discipler, and his primary disciples are seated at his dinner table every day. Remember, one of the most important roles of Elijah the prophet, besides speaking the Word of God to Israel, was to train the man of God who came after him. Elijah discipled Elisha who then mentored others under him after Elijah was translated into glory. That's the pattern of discipleship that is to be followed in our homes as well. Again, Ephesians 6:4 says we dads are to bring our children up "in the training and admonition of the Lord." This must be our conviction. We have to believe that our primary disciples really are our children, and it must be a conviction, not a preference, or we will not take it seriously. How do we do this? Let's look at Jesus' example of disciple-making: "Then He appointed twelve, that they might be with Him and that He might send them out to preach" (Mark 3:14). Discipleship starts by being *with* our children as Jesus was *with* His disciples. He was intent on equipping them to send them out. They saw Jesus' passion for the Father in everything He said and in everything He did. That shaped the twelve and equipped them for ministry. Have you ever thought about the fact that your ministry as a father is to equip your children to send them out to preach? Though they may never stand in a church pulpit, they will "preach" every day of their lives with words and deeds. And the passion with which they preach will have been caught from you, their father.

D.A. Carson said, "If I have learned anything in 35 or 40 years of teaching, it is that students don't learn everything I teach them. What they learn is what I am excited about, the kinds of things I emphasize again and again and again and again. That had better be the gospel." (spoken in a lecture at the CBMW Different by Design Conference, Feb. 2, 2009, Minneapolis, MN)

This simply means that the mechanics of what we do and how we disciple pales in comparison with the importance of our own passion. We can go through discipleship materials until the cows come home or until the children leave home, whichever comes first, and it will be an exercise in futility if they don't see a passion for the Gospel in our own lives. So, get a passion for God, and if you don't have one, pray until you do. Read the Bible until you do. Go to church and worship with others who have a passion for God until you do, too.

Here are some things you can do with your children, fueled by a passion for the Gospel. Spend time going through a book with them, one on one or as a group. Teach them to pray. Play games with them. Spend time having fun with your children. The truth is, many fathers are too consumed with their own lives to enter into the world of their children and just have fun with them. You may have heard this example, but it bears repeating: "Brooks Adams, a boy who lived in the 19th century kept a diary, which is still in existence. On one day in his childhood, Brooks Adams made this entry: "Went fishing with my father, the most wonderful day of my life!" Curious about this event, someone went and found the diary of Brooks' father, Charles Francis Adams, a famous political figure and diplomat. On that same day, he entered: "Went fishing with my son today, a day wasted." What a sad testimony, and one that is repeated often in Christian families all across the nation.

I love being with my children, whether we are just watching a ballgame together on TV or doing something that requires more energy and planning, like a camping trip. And it is sometimes what we did not plan for, but experienced together, that makes the greatest memories.

A recent weekend for the Fox men was meticulously planned. Well, let me qualify that. It was about as planned as it could be by my standards. My motto is, "If I get there and I don't have it, well, that's what Wal-Mart is for." My wife's motto is, "If I am leaving the house and I have forgotten something, then the four checklists, six spreadsheets, and four days of planning that would rival the preparation for D-Day were not enough." I am kidding about Cindy, but some of you men will recognize this statement as you are backing out of the garage to go on vacation or even just to church, "I just feel like I have forgotten something." She often looks at me as she says it, and I will say, "Of course you feel that way, darling. But you never do forget anything. And if you did, well, that's what Wal-Mart is for."

This weekend trip was just my five sons and me, and we were headed for the mountains to camp, cook over the open fire, laugh a lot, and talk about our lives. The campsite was a little over two hours away from home, and about fifteen miles from our destination the transmission started to give up the ghost. That's what I forgot to bring, I thought: a spare transmission! All the rental car places were closed, so we limped back toward Burlington, thinking that if the transmission was going to die completely, the closer to home we were, the better.

Four hours later, we arrived at a lake lot owned by a family in the church, just twenty miles from home, and tried to pick the lock to the Dutch barn on their property, with their permission of course. That's another thing our spreadsheet failed to include, a lock-pick. We gave up after an hour and decided to pitch our tent in the dark. I wasn't worried about sleeping; my friend Mark had loaned us their tent and a queen size air mattress. I realized as we were setting up camp that I forgot a pump. The prospect of two hours of blowing up the mattress left me feeling breathless, and there wasn't a Wal-Mart in sight, so I slept on the queen-size sheets.

We built a fire, ate s'mores, and talked about college,

relationships, jobs, and future plans. The next day, we had planned to drive north a few miles to play disc golf. That plan was changed when we realized the transmission had not been healed as we slept, so we started toward home. A twenty-mile trip took an hour and included some scenes worthy of a sit-com episode as Micah drove while the rest of us jumped out and pushed the van up hills then made a mad dash to jump back into the moving vehicle. Don't try this at home or even in Caswell County.

We traded the van in for two worthier vehicles back at the house and still got in three hours of disc golf. Judah said later, "That was the best day of my life."

This camping trip will go down in the Foxian chronicles and be told for generations. It was not at all what we planned but it was everything we needed, and a powerful reminder that "A man's heart plans his way, but the Lord directs his steps" (Proverbs 16:9). We can trust Him for a camping trip, for a college career, for a marriage decision, and for every other step we take.

It's often the unplanned that makes the best memories. Still, next time we're taking Micah's car.

~~~

Here's another idea for discipleship: go on a mission

trip together. I cannot begin to put a price tag on the mission trips I have been on with my children. Five of the seven have been to Africa with me and accompanied me as I taught a pastors' conference, ministering to the children at the same time I was teaching the men. Two of my sons and one of my daughters have been to Haiti with me. This past year, I had the privilege of taking my wife and four of our children to Colombia, South America. As we were leaving at 4:00 a.m. to go to the airport, my wife said, "This is the first time in twenty-five years I haven't had to say goodbye." What a powerful blessing we enjoyed as a family to serve the body of Christ on the little island of Bocachica. Priceless discipleship.

So, a prophet hears from God, communicates what he has heard to his family, and disciples his children. There is one last thing he must do.

A prophet must provide correction and discipline when necessary. Remember this role of the prophet? He would even correct and discipline a wayward king, if needed. Nathan confronted King David with his sins. Elijah confronted King Ahab and Queen Jezebel. Paul said we are to bring up our children "in the training and admonition of the Lord." Admonition is a word that means, "to put into the mind." Spiros Zhodiates says admonition includes, "a word of encouragement when it proves sufficient, but also by a word or action that reproves and corrects." Proverbs 29:17 says, "Correct your son, and he will give you rest; yes, he will give delight to your soul." Sometimes my job as a dad meant that I put something into my young child's mind by drawing his attention sharply to another area of his body. J

I think one of the ways we provoke a child to anger is by not correcting and disciplining. Mark Gregston of Heartlight Ministries believes that children and teens need rules, boundaries, and beliefs to be clearly spelled out in the home. He says, "When a teenager doesn't know what is expected in your home, he does what seems right in his own eyes-and that's a formula for chaos." (www.heartlightministries.org/blogs/markgregston/2007/09/22) Perhaps they interpret this as indifference, which translates to them that they are not loved.

Not only do our children, and especially our sons, want and need to be disciplined to know that they are loved, they want and need to be challenged as well. I love the story of the high school assembly where the three recruiters were there to try to sign up young men for their respective branches. There was an Army recruiter, a Navy recruiter, and a Marine recruiter. They were told by the principal before the assembly, "You men will each get five minutes at the end of the assembly to make your appeal for recruits, and then those interested in hearing more can meet with you in the cafeteria where you have your tables set up." They agreed to the time limit, but at the end of the assembly, the Army recruiter got up and spoke for eight minutes. The Navy recruiter, realizing what had happened, kept his talk to six minutes. But the Marine recruiter looked over at the principal, who looked at his watch and signaled to the Marine, ONE minute. He had ONE minute. You know what he did? He stood there at the podium for a full forty-five seconds, staring out at the high school students seated before him. Didn't say a word for forty-five seconds. Then he said, "If any of you think you have the *guts* to be a Marine, see me in the cafeteria after the assembly." Then he sat down. When the three recruiters walked into the cafeteria a few minutes later, there were two or three students waiting to talk to the Army recruiter, and two or three waiting to talk to the Navy recruiter, and 106 waiting to talk to the Marine. The reason was simple. He challenged them. And young men want to be challenged.

If we emphasize this last duty of a prophet, to discipline and correct, at the expense of the first two duties, to teach and to train, we will provoke our children to wrath, the very thing Paul tells us not to do. Or we will drive our children to discouragement. I will write more about this in the next section, "Men as Priests."

Part Two: Faithful Men as Priests

Chapter 7
Proclaiming His praises to my family

Todd Wilson of FamilyMan Ministries says his motto is "I'm a pretty good dad...except when I'm not." (www.familymanweb.com) I think that we could all relate to that. We could all say "Hey, I'm a pretty good dad... except when I'm not. I'm a pretty good husband...except when I'm not. I'm a pretty good brother to my brothers in Christ...except when I'm not." The fact is that we're all in process...none of us has arrived. That is true of us as prophets in our homes, and it is certainly true of us as priests. A priest is someone who leads, who stands up front and is moving toward God. The same is true of a husband and a father.

The primary responsibility of the man is to lead his family in a way that directs them toward Christ. That means that two dynamics are working together for God's glory. One, the man is actively pursuing Christ with all his heart himself. Two, he is intentionally guiding his family toward that same goal. Zig Ziglar said, "If you aim at nothing, you will hit it every time." If we are aiming at nothing, those who observe us with our families in public will be able to tell that our children have been left to their own devices. "A child left *to himself,*" Proverbs says, "brings shame to his mother" (29:15). The person who sees us in a restaurant and hears the disrespect in our children's voices, or senses the iciness in the conversation of husband and wife, will note, "In that home it's clear that there's a lack of headship." They may not say it, but they will sense it; they will know that there is trouble, that there's a head there, but he's not doing or has not done what is clearly required of him. Somewhere he has dropped the ball, and in fact, that's why the family is struggling so much.

Let's consider what it means to be the priest of your home, men. We know that Peter makes it clear that all believers are part of the royal priesthood. "But you *are* a chosen generation, a royal priesthood, a holy nation, His own special people, that you may proclaim the praises of Him who called you out of darkness into His marvelous light" (1 Peter 2:9). As men and women, we have the same standing in Christ, as Peter clearly says and Paul affirms in Galatians 3:28, "There is neither Jew nor Greek, there is neither slave nor free, there is neither male nor female; for you are all one in Christ Jesus." We have the same standing as men and women, and in one sense, we are all priests who have been invited into the holy of holies. But Paul makes it clear in 1 Corinthians 11:3, as we have seen already, that men and women do not have the same roles in the church or the home. Men are called to lead, and it is in the capacity as leader in the home that I believe a man needs to understand his distinct responsibilities as a priest.

First, *the priest goes before the people on behalf of God.* Why do we do that? Peter explains why in verse nine: "that you may proclaim the praises of Him who called you out of darkness." We are called as priests to go before the people in our houses on behalf of God to proclaim His praises, to teach and to demonstrate by our own lives how precious, how wonderful, how awesome God really is. You've heard it said before, but it bears repeating that the children in your household, especially your sons, are going to think of God the way they think of their dad. Children who grow up with a father who is silent when it comes to matters of faith, but vocal when it comes to his job or his money or his hobbies will be shaped by that, and their values will mirror their father's values. Dad, you are a mirror, you're a reflector, if you will, of what God is like. Your sons and your daughters look at you and see someone who reflects the Father...or someone who is not necessarily doing that. Think about that with regard to the priest in the Old Testament. If there was anything that put a priest in good standing before God and His people, it was the fact that the priest loved the Lord and was faithful to keep *that relationship* in the forefront of his ministry. When a priest faithfully executed his duties in the Old Testament out of a heart of love for God, there was a blessing on him, his family, and on all of the people under his care. When a priest let his responsibilities go or abdicated his responsibilities or violated his responsibilities before God, there was not only a curse on him and his family, there was also a curse on those who followed him.

Think of the judgment that came on Eli because he did not restrain his sons from doing evil. This priest of Israel was not faithful in his own home; as a result, his sons died in battle, the nation was defeated by the Philistines, and the ark of God was stolen! Eli's grandson was born at the news that his father had been killed in battle, and his mother named him Ichabod, meaning "the glory has departed" (1 Samuel 4:21). It was a sad day in Israel, and it could have been prevented had Eli been a faithful father. Men lost their lives, and the nation lost its glory because of one man's disobedience. Perhaps the stakes are not quite that high for us, but are they not high enough to provoke us to live as faithful leaders in our homes? If the spiritual health and well-being of our own children are not enough to exhort us, then we are deadened by our own sinful flesh, as Eli was.

Another example gives us a positive model to follow.

Ezra served as a priest during the time of Israel's captivity in Babylon and the period immediately following the return to Jerusalem. Before Nehemiah was sent to rebuild the walls of Jerusalem, Ezra went to lead in the restoration of worship in the holy city. Ezra 7:9 says, "On the first *day* of the first month he began *his* journey from Babylon, and on the first *day* of the fifth month he came to Jerusalem, according to the good hand of his God upon him." I love that phrase. How many of you want the good hand of God upon you as priests in your homes? Of course we all want that, don't we?

We could ask the question, *why* was the good hand of God upon Ezra? The answer appears, I believe, in the next verse. "For Ezra had prepared his heart to seek the Law of the Lord, and to do *it*, and to teach statutes and ordinances in Israel" (7:10). That is a powerful combination, a threefold cord, if you will, that is not easily broken. First, Ezra sought the Word of God. We are told in an earlier verse that Ezra was "a skilled scribe in the Law of Moses, which the Lord God of Israel had given" (7:6). Ezra had honed his skill in the Word over years of study. He had become an expert in it. I would imagine that when someone had a question about the Law of Moses, the first five books of the Bible, they went to Ezra. I am convinced, however, that they would not have gone to him were it not for the second part of this threefold cord, "to do it."

Ezra set his heart to do the Word, not just to study it and to know it. Can you really say, after all, that you *know* the Word if you do not do it? The Hebrew understanding of "knowing" was experiential; it meant that you knew something because you had lived it, experienced it.

I can tell my children about skydiving, because I know from study and hearing second-hand reports how it works and what it means to skydive. But if one of my children really wants to *know* skydiving, they need to talk to someone who has done more than study it or read about it. They want to talk to someone who has jumped out of a perfectly good airplane...and lived to tell about it.

When my wife was pregnant with our first child, she didn't go to the young ladies she had grown up with and ask them about childbirth, because they had not experienced it yet. She sought out women in our church who had given birth. She wanted information from those who had lived it. The good hand of God is upon men and women who have set their hearts both to study and to do the Word of God. The question is not, how much have you been through the Bible? The real question is, how much has the Bible been through you? When we are considering a man in our church for possible appointment as an elder, we want to know that he has developed a lifestyle of reading the Bible and meditating on its truth. Along with that, we are looking at his life and listening to his speech to see if he really is *in* the Word and the Word is *in* him. When he prays, does he pray Bible? When he counsels others, does he counsel Bible? If we cut him, will he bleed Bible?

I was speaking to a group of college students and had a cup of water in my hand that was almost full to the brim. I requested a volunteer to come up front, and when a young lady stepped forward, I asked her to hold the cup. Then I started talking and while gesturing I bumped her hand, causing about a third of the water to slosh out and create a puddle on the floor. Frowning as if I were really disappointed, I inquired, "Kelly, why did water come out of that cup?"

She laughed nervously, "Because you bumped my hand!"

I grinned slightly and replied, "Oh, I see, it's *my* fault. It's always somebody else's fault, is that it, Kelly?" She laughed, a little more nervously, and I added, "No, Kelly, let's think of another reason. Why did water come out of that cup?"

She paused a moment, "Um, well, because it was really full."

Again, I just smiled a little and replied, "Oh, OK, now you're going to use science on me. Like, you know, Mark, if you fill a cup to the top, and the equilibrium of the cup is compromised, then there will be spillage." I shook my head and laughed, "No, Kelly, that's not the right answer. One more try. Why did water come out of that cup?"

Kelly looked at her feet and then back at me and shook her head while quietly mouthing, "I don't know." I smiled, thanked her, and we gave her a big round of applause.

As she walked back to her seat I explained, "You know why water came out of that cup? Because water is what was *in* the cup. When you get bumped, what comes out of you? Whatever is on the inside comes out. That's why Jesus said, 'Out of the abundance of the heart the mouth speaks'" (Matthew 12:34).

Ezra had prepared his heart to study and to do the Word of God. He was the real deal, and therefore his ministry enjoyed the blessing of God. One more illustration. I have used this one in a number of different settings, even with a group of one hundred pastors in the middle of nowhere in Kenya. I start by asking the group to raise their right hand. That's always a challenge, no matter the gathering, so I usually have to say, "No, your other right hand." Then I ask everyone to make a circle by touching the tips of their right thumb and right index finger together. "Ok, now take that circle and place it on your cheek." As I say that, I take my "circle" and place it on my *chin*, not my cheek. More than 90% of the people in the room will do the same; they will place their circle on their chin, even though I told them plainly to put it on their cheek! It is proof, I tell them, that we believe much more what we see than what we hear. A father who tells his children that they should read the Bible every day and learn to love the Word of God, and then demonstrates by his actions that he really doesn't have time for the Bible and rarely speaks about it other than to tell his children they need to read it, will communicate much more powerfully by his actions than by his words. His children will do what they see, not what they hear. They will hear *cheek* but see *chin*, and *chin* it will be! This is not cliché; truth really is more *caught* than *taught* with our children. Our children will believe what we profess if they see that it is truly what we possess.

Ezra not only had a heart that was prepared, he not only studied the Word so that he knew it and had a word from God to proclaim, but he was faithfully carrying out the Word of the Lord in front of the people. And I believe that communicated volumes to the people of God. They watched their priest and thought, "This man loves God. You can tell, not just by what he says, but by the way he lives."

The person in my childhood who stands out as an Ezra to me, someone who demonstrated a love for God in everything she said and did, was my Great-Grandma Hauser. She was a tiny woman with a big heart, gray hair she kept pulled back in a bun, and calloused knees from years spent in prayer. But what I remember most about Grandma Hauser were her hands. They were little hands, with blue veins that looked like they were coming through the skin, and age spots, but oh how those little hands could work, serve, and love!

I can still see her kneeling at her bed, her dog-eared Reference Bible at her side, her hands folded reverently as she talked to her best Friend in prayer. I can still feel the sting of those same hands when Grandma would deliver one of her well-deserved pops to my backside. And I can still remember the day those hands saved my life. Grandma Hauser had given me a Life Saver®, and I got carried away eating it and swallowed the whole thing. It lodged in my windpipe, and I began to choke and gag, and my 70-year-old Grandma smacked me on the back, putting all of her 98 pounds into it. The Life Saver® popped out, and the breath came back in.

I can see her in the kitchen, working with her hands, warming up some tomato soup for my brothers and me on a December day when it was too cold to be outside, but was just right in her house. I can see her sitting on her settee, as she called it, her little hands working the blue crochet needles, her voice humming one of her favorite hymns. I can feel her hands as she rubbed a little boy's back as I lay real still beside her on the couch, afraid that if I moved, she would stop.

I remember the story of the time Grandma was in church, and the offering plate was being passed. She picked up the purse next to her, opened it up and searched for the gift she had prepared that morning for the Lord's work. But it wasn't there! Grandma Hauser's hands moved faster as she rifled through that purse, and she got more frustrated when she couldn't find her offering envelope. All the while, the plate was getting closer, and the lady sitting next to Grandma was tugging at her sleeve, whispering, "Jessie, Jessie."

Grandma then dumped the entire contents of the purse there on the pew and muttered under her breath, "If the Lord lets me live to get back home, *I'm going to clean this pocketbook out!*" Finally the lady next to her got Grandma's attention and declared, "Jessie, that's *my* pocketbook!"

Whether she was praying, disciplining, cooking, or crocheting, Grandma's hands were always busy doing something for someone else. And one day when I was fifteen years old, I saw Grandma's hands folded across her chest for the last time. I touched them, and they had lost their warmth, and the life no longer animated them to serve or spank or pray. But I can take comfort in two things. Grandma's first sight with new eyes was the face and the nail-scarred hands of the Master she had loved and lived for. That makes me smile. And the second thing that comforts me is that I know one day I will see Grandma Hauser again. I will thank her as an adult, like I never did as a child, for her hands of love that meant so much to me.

The third strand of the threefold cord is this: Ezra prepared his heart to teach the Word of God. Because Ezra knew it, and because Ezra lived it, Ezra could teach it. In fact, Ezra could not *not* teach it. By the very way he lived it out before them, Ezra taught his fellow Israelites the truths of God's Word. That does not mean that he did not have to say anything, or that he just "lived a quiet testimony to the Lord in front of the people." Maybe you have heard someone say something like this, "I believe the most important thing is that we live our faith, you know, like Francis of Assisi who said, 'Preach the Gospel always; when necessary, use words.'" To begin with, that quote is most likely unfairly attributed to St. Francis. It did not appear until two centuries after his death, *and* St.

Francis was known for bold proclamations of the truth of the Gospel. Whoever first said it, the truth is that many times the attitude behind this statement is this, "There is *no* way I am ever going to confront someone with the Word of God! There is *no* way I am going to stand up in front of any group and presume to teach them anything. There is *no* way I am even going to try and tell one person, even a close friend, how they should live their life. I mean, who does that sort of thing?" Well, Ezra did that sort of thing. And if you are going to be a faithful priest in your own house, then *you* have to do that sort of thing. More on that in a moment.

It would be a good thing for all of us to memorize Ezra 7:10, to meditate on it, to study it, and to really get it down in our souls. When you walk in the reality of this threefold cord, you extend the blessing of God not only to your family, but beyond. You will increase your sphere of influence. You've heard it said before: we are responsible for the depth of our ministry, the depth of our heart, the depth of our soul—God is responsible for the breadth. When we take care of the depth—seeking the Lord, knowing His Word, doing His Word, teaching His Word—He expands the breadth. Look at Ezra 7:28b. Ezra says, "So I was encouraged, as the hand of the Lord my God *was* upon me; and I gathered leading men of Israel to go up with me." How could he have gathered leading men of Israel if, in fact, he did not have integrity before them? They respected him, they trusted him, they wanted to follow him. Ezra could not *command* them to come, he *asked* them to come, and they wanted to.

So, men, what you're doing right now in your family is going to make a difference in your family, in your church family, and in the community you live in. In fact, it might even make a difference around the world. I can tell you that the things I have learned and practiced in my own family have become the platform from which I can speak to men in our congregation and to men in other settings like conferences, even to men in other countries; I have shared some or all of this material in Kenya, Zimbabwe, and Ghana, with pastors and church leaders who have then taken these truths and shared them with their congregations. God takes care of the breadth as we commit to going deeper and walking in obedience.

Ezra had opportunity to speak some hard truths from God's Word to the people of God. Men from the tribes of Judah and Benjamin gathered in Jerusalem to hear from Ezra, as recorded in Ezra 10. All of the men sat in the open square of the house of God, even though it was pouring down rain. That reminds me of the story of one of David's mighty men who killed a lion in a pit on a snowy day (1 Chronicles 11:22). Vance Havner said something like, "That is amazing, considering it's hard to get a deacon out of bed on a rainy Sunday morning." The men of Judah and Benjamin gathered in the pouring rain to hear the Word, and that's when Ezra took out the big hammer of God's law and thundered against them. Read Ezra 9 and see what had happened in Israel during the time of the Babylonian captivity, during the time when the people were living in shame. They were beginning to intermarry. The men of Israel disobeyed God and married pagans. When Ezra heard of this national disgrace, the first thing he did was pray and confess the sins of his people, "Now while Ezra was praying, and while he was confessing" (10:1). This is the second major responsibility of the priests in the Old Testament; they went before God on behalf of the people.

Chapter 8
Worship On!

The priest went before God on behalf of his people, foremost as a worshiper. Who led the worship in the temple? The priests. Who was trained and set apart by God to take the people into worship? The priests. Who is to be the worship leader in our homes? Dad. Who is set apart by God to lead his family into worship? The husband and father. Who is the worship leader of your family as we gather for corporate worship on Sunday morning? You are! There may be a man in front of the congregation who is leading the music at the piano or with his guitar, but you are the worship leaders, men. Your family will learn to worship and learn to love to worship as they watch and imitate you. Let me ask you, then, how much do you enjoy singing praise songs to the Lord? Do your children see you singing with all your heart, worshiping the Lord like David did, "with all your might," or do they have to look around and find someone else to imitate?

As they carried the ark of the Lord back to where it belonged, with King David leading, the people of Israel stopped every six steps and worshiped. A sacrifice was made of oxen and fatted sheep. David was making sure that God was honored in this procession, and that the hearts of the people were turned toward the Lord. They had tried to bring the ark of the Lord back once before, on a cart rather than on the shoulders of priests, as God had prescribed. It did not go well. This time, David followed God's instructions, and the procession slowly wound toward Jerusalem. The sacrifices were made every six steps, but something else marked the joyful procession as well. David danced. The literal translation in 2 Samuel 6:14 is that David "twirled around." It wasn't a choreographed exhibition that David had worked on in the privacy of his chambers, with an ancestor of Martha Graham or Rudolf Nureyev. No, this was a spontaneous outburst of unabashed joy, expressed through David's feet and his entire body. Before the Lord. That's a key phrase in the passage. David danced before the Lord. For an audience of one. His was not a carefully planned scheme to show off his versatility for the Israeli people. "Look at me, I can dance!" He was not auditioning for the Hebrews' new season of *Dancing with the Stars*. He was not trying to overcome a boyish fear of the spotlight by doing the most absurdly brash thing he could think of at the time. No. In fact, David was not thinking of David at all. He danced before the Lord. Not only that, David danced before the Lord "with all his might." He threw away man's predilection to do just enough to get by. David danced before the Lord with abandon. Why? It was worship. Dancing is so often not worship, but here it was. David worshiped the Lord with the dance, just as Psalm 149:3 says.

I will make two observations about this story and the encouragement in Psalms. One, I realize that dancing in the worship service is most likely not a part of your tradition. Indeed, it is not what I am used to seeing, at least not in this culture. Go with me to Kenya or Zimbabwe, though, and your understanding of what is "normal" in worship will be challenged. The point is, worship is not defined by particular actions, but by the heart attitude. David danced before the Lord with all his might. He could have sung with all his might, and that would make many of you feel a little better about this whole episode. But he danced. He could have yodeled, and that would make us even more uncomfortable, wouldn't it? I cannot picture the Kenyans breaking out into a group yodel at the top of their lungs.

Two, David's wife, Michal, didn't think much of his dancing. In fact, the Bible says she looked out a window at David and saw him twirling with abandon, and "she despised him in her heart" (1 Samuel 6:16). Sadly, there are many Michals in the church today who stand back sneering at those who worship the Lord with more emotion or movement or even joy than they. Like Michal, they miss the celebration of God in worship themselves because of their own judgmental spirit.

The truth is, worship invites warfare. When you worship the living God, you draw a line in the sand and declare your allegiance. That will provoke the believers to exultation and the faithless to condemnation.

Worship on.

Men, you are the worship leaders in your home, and your leadership will be on display Sunday morning as you stand with your family to sing praises to the Lord. But Sunday morning is greatly affected by Saturday night, and by every day leading up to it that week. It takes preparation for us to be ready to worship. The regulations and ordinances in Leviticus that prescribed how worship was to be prepared for and carried out by the priest provide us with a physical picture of a spiritual reality. Taking people into worship means preparation and responsibility. How much preparation goes into getting your family ready to worship on Sunday morning? You can prepare the hearts of your wife and children to worship corporately on Sunday by demonstrating worship all week in the family. Give God glory. Praise Him in front of your family. Lead daily devotions with an attitude that God is awesome. Come to church with expectation, and talk about that on the way. Pray for the worship team as a family as you drive in. Pray for the pastor and the other elders as they prepare to lead and minister to the flock. Prepare to worship God.

I found this in a blog by Wes Thorp. I don't know the man, but I appreciate his thoughts about preparing for worship:

"I'm waiting in line to use the shower in our busy little household as we get ready to go to church. It's a perfect time for me to get my head and heart in a right place where I am ready to meet God . . . I find it too easy to breeze into church, get a cup of coffee, sit down and let it happen.

I know that I need to position myself to be open to God and His love. I have to be ready to receive it.

Oswald Chambers from his devotional book *My Ut-most for His Highest* writes about being Christ aware, rather than self-aware. I find it too easy to focus on (the) circumstances of the present whether in politics or in the culture (more than) Jesus Christ and who He is, what He has done and continues to do." (http://westhorp.type-pad.com/dailygrit/2011/08/getting-ready-for-church-on-this-sunday-morning-late-in-august.html)

Second, the priest went before God on behalf of the people of God as an intercessor. Hebrews 7:25 states that Jesus, who is our High Priest forever, "always lives to make intercession." As Christ is seated beside the Father as our High Priest, forever making intercession for His children, we also are given that great honor and privilege. Pray for your wife. Pray for your children. Bring them before the throne of grace every day, asking the Lord to bless them and to keep them. Get to know what your wife and children are struggling with and pray for them about that. It is certainly important to pray about the sin we see in our family. And if there is a spiritual attack going on, you have more authority than anyone else in the whole world to deal with it.

There was a time, early in our marriage, when Cindy

struggled mightily with fear, sometimes irrational fear. The enemy was attacking our marriage through her fear, no question about it, but mostly I was too blind or impatient or selfish to see it. I would get frustrated with her and scold her for letting fear get the best of her. "Come on! You know we have not been given a spirit of fear!" I would say to her. My quoting Scripture to my wife somehow just didn't do the trick. It all came to a head one day when we were having a couple from South Africa over for lunch. He was visiting a ministry in the area that we were connected with, and we had agreed to entertain them. The man was a general in the South African military, and the last thing we wanted to do was to mess this up. Cindy got so upset over the details of getting ready for the luncheon that she suddenly went blank. Her brain just shut down, perhaps as a way of coping with the enormous amount of stress she was experiencing. It scared me to death. I cried out to the Lord for her, and she got better, and we limped through the lunch date with the general and his wife. But the incident prompted us to get biblical counseling, and it prompted me to get serious about praying for my wife. The turning point came for her one day when I laid my hands on her head and began to pray for her deliverance from fear. I submitted to the Lord, resisted the devil (James 4:7), and asked that God would cause him to flee. Cindy felt a release in her spirit, and the tide turned after that. The panic attacks ceased. Cindy grew tremendously through this whole ordeal, and there were still some struggles along the way, but she was not crippled again by fear. She has told the story many times to encourage women, and she points to the prayer of her husband as a turning point. I have told men many times as well that no one on the planet has as much authority for mighty, effectual prayer over their wives as they do.

The ministry of prayer is perhaps the most important ministry we will ever have with our children, also. It is a lifelong ministry, for one thing, because even after they move out, get married, and set up their own households, we still need to uphold them in prayer. While they are under our roof, we definitely have a ministry of prayer that can be powerful in its effect and profound in its fruitfulness. Paul Miller says in his excellent book, *A Praying Life,* that the most important parenting he ever did was through prayer. It is a wise father who serves his family by spending time at God's throne every day, praying for his wife and children and interceding on their behalf.

I ask every morning during family devotions, "What do we need to pray about?" It is important to give your children and wife the opportunity to tell you what concerns them, what is coming up that day or that week that they need the Lord's help with. I would love to say that all of my children come to me regularly with things they want me to pray about. Sometimes they do, and it thrills my soul. There needs to be the freedom for them to do that, even to interrupt you at work or home with a need to talk or to share a prayer request.

One of my memories of our oldest son is when he was in the 14 to 16-year-old range. I would be in bed, trying to read a sentence for the fifth time, nodding off, about to turn off the light to go to sleep, and I would hear a little tap on the door jamb. Micah would be standing there, looking a little nervous, and he would say, "Dad, can I talk to you about something?" It was usually something he was struggling with in his thought life, and Micah wanted to clear his conscience and get assurance from me that he was OK. He also wanted to know that I was praying for him. Those moments helped build a strong relationship that continues to this day. Now married and the father of two, Micah will still come to me with his struggles sometimes and ask me to pray for him. What a treasure!

I wrote a newspaper column several years ago about my relationship with my oldest son entitled "A Glad Father Enjoys the Fruits of His Labor."

Last week I had the opportunity to spend the better part of an afternoon with a good friend of mine. I was flying to Kenya and had a six-hour layover in Detroit. So, my friend came and picked me up at the airport. We found a little cafe close by, and had a pleasant lunch together. Then we asked directions to the nearest Starbucks, and spent another two hours there, enjoying the fact that neither one of us had to be anywhere that afternoon, there was nothing pressing us, and we could simply enjoy the company, the wonderful smell of coffee brewing, and the laughter of good friends.

We talked easily of old times, swapped stories, joked around, and just enjoyed being together. I reflected later on the plane how much I love this friend of mine, and look forward to the next time we can be together. The funny thing is, though we have known each other for 21 years, our relationship has changed drastically in the last two.

You see, this friend is also my oldest son. Micah attends college about an hour from Detroit, and was able to come down and hang out with Dad for half a day. We talked about the courses he is taking in college and the things he is learning about life. We discussed the job offer he has waiting for him after he graduates this May. We laughed about college pranks, and we agonized together about the Panther's loss to Seattle. We talked about theology and about career choices and about marriage.

When Micah dropped me off at the airport and we hugged, it felt as natural and as easy to say "I love you" to my son as anything I have ever done.

What a blessing! I felt like I was sitting down to a banquet of fresh fruits and vegetables that my wife and I had planted in a different season. All of the agony of back-breaking toil in the hot sun was forgotten because the harvest was in, and the feast was prepared. The labor was eclipsed by the sweet reward. The fruit was delicious and satisfying.

I am not writing this to point to myself as a good father. Believe me when I say that I have made as many mistakes as anyone. I remember a basketball game that almost came to blows because of my own pride and stubborn competitiveness. Micah's cooler head prevailed, and we were spared what could have been a devastating blow to our relationship. I remember many times when I disciplined in anger. I remember several years of awkward embarrassment between us as he grew into manhood, and the hugs were fewer than they should have been, the expressions of love forced at times, absent at others. I remember the times I didn't do the thing my son needed, and the times I did or said the wrong thing. But I am eternally grateful, and I give praise to the One who is able to take my meager efforts and my mistakes and redeem them for His own glorious purposes. He has certainly done that in my relationship with Micah. And I trust God will do the same with each of my children.

The Bible says, "A wise son makes a glad father, but a foolish son *is* the grief of his mother" (Proverbs 10:1).

This is one glad father.

Chapter 9
Keeping It Real

I thank God for the grace He freely gives us dads to build strong relationships with our children. I encourage you to begin to build an atmosphere in your home that communicates to the family that you love them unconditionally and will pray for them about anything they ask you to. Then do it.

That's what we find Ezra doing in chapter ten of the book that bears his name, confessing the sins of the people under his care. The priests would confess the sins of the people in their "household," even if they personally did not commit the sins of their household. The man of the house, though he is not guilty of the sins his children commit, bears responsibility as the head of his house. Ezra was praying, and while he was "confessing, weeping, and bowing down before the house of God, a very large assembly of men, women, and children gathered to him from Israel; for the people wept very bitterly. And Shechaniah

. . . said to Ezra, 'We have trespassed against our God, and have taken pagan wives from the peoples of the land; yet now there is hope in Israel in spite of this.'" (Ezra 10:1-2) Then something incredible happens. Ezra begins to hold the men of God accountable for their actions. He has gone before the people on behalf of God, and he takes action to hold them responsible for their sins. He names their sin and commands them to confess it and renounce it.

"Then the descendants of the captivity did so. And Ezra the priest, *with* certain heads of the fathers' households, were set apart by the fathers' households, each of them by name; and they sat down on the first day of the tenth month to examine the matter. By the first day of the first month they finished *questioning* all the men who had taken pagan wives. And among the sons of the priests who had taken pagan wives *the following* were found of the sons of Jeshua the son of Jozadak, and his brothers: Maaseiah, Eliezer, Jarib, and Gedaliah. And they gave their promise that they would put away their wives; and *being* guilty, *they presented* a ram of the flock as their trespass offering." (Ezra 10:16-19)

This is so important, men. Do you see the steps Ezra took as a priest over the household of Israel?

1. He sat down with his people.
2. He examined the matter.
3. He asked questions.
4. He found the truth.

It reminds me of that church trip to a youth conference in my fifteenth year, when we were caught planning to buy alcohol and spend the week indulging the flesh. The revival that took place in the hearts of a handful of young people that week started when the pastor met individually with each one of us to hold us accountable. He knew that cleansing starts with confession. Blessing comes from brokenness. The Lord will crush a man before He crowns him. Do you see all of that? Don't miss the final point from Ezra 10:19.

5. He saw it through to repentance.

Let me ask you something, Dad. Do you know your children? Do you know them well enough to know if they are pursuing a relationship with the Lord? You may know, second-hand, because you rely on your wife to tell you how the kids are doing in school, in the Word, in their chores, and you are just too busy to keep up with all of that. If that's the case, I suggest that you are too busy. To function effectively as the priest of your house that God has called you to be may mean that something else has got to go. Do you ever sit down with your children and help them examine their walk with the Lord? Do you ask them questions about their faith and about their walk? One of the best times to do that is when you're riding in your car with one of them alone. Turn off the radio, turn off the iPod, turn off the music, and certainly turn off the TV if you happen to have one of those in the car, and tell them to take the plugs out of their ears...then, have a conversation, and ask questions! I will often ask one of my sons as we're driving back from church, "What did you learn from the sermon today?" Or I might say, "What are you learning from the Lord these days?" Or I may ask, "How's it going? Anything on your mind that you want to talk about?" I like Eric Wallace's questions that he uses for men's accountability. They are, "How's your heart? How's your life? What's your plan? How can I help?"

Sometimes we need to be pointed in our questions with our children. Do you ask them questions about the sin that you see in their lives? The inconsistencies, the rebellions, the brokenness? And do you stay with it, with them, all the way through to repentance? This is a crucial responsibility that we have as priests in our own homes, but the sad reality, men, is that many times we're too busy. We are either too busy pursuing our own dreams, our own goals, building our empire, building our wealth, building our portfolio, working ninety hours a week, whatever, that we don't take time to sit down with our children and find these things out. Or, we are too ashamed to sit down with our children and find out how they're doing because we are not doing so well ourselves. We have to make sure we've got that beam out of our own eyes. Guys, with us it's always a beam—just keep this in mind, with us it's always a beam—with our children, it's always a speck. If you flip-flop that thing around and think your son's got a beam you've got to pull out of his head, then you're going to do great damage to your relationship with your son. First take the log out of your own eye, and then you can sit down with your son or your daughter and say, "Hey, let's talk about this thing you're struggling with." Stay with it all the way through to repentance.

We have seen so far that the priest went before his people as a worshiper and as an intercessor. He also went before God to ask for wisdom concerning the people of God. One of the rebukes of God to the shepherds in Israel was, "My sheep wandered through all the mountains, and on every high hill; yes, My flock was scattered over the whole face of the earth, and no one was seeking or searching *for them*" (Ezekiel. 34:6). We need to seek and search out where our wives and children are spiritually. Do your children know Jesus, and are they pursuing a relationship with Him? Is your wife in a good place, or is she wandering over the face of the earth trying to figure out what she should be doing? We can let our wives wander into all sorts of things simply because we say, "I want her to be happy." What's more important than her being happy is that she is doing exactly what God would have her to do. A priest seeks the Lord for wisdom so he can give guidance, even if it means saying something that will not be popular in his wife's eyes or in his children's eyes.

Finally, a priest also gave his people a blessing.

And the LORD spoke to Moses, saying, "Speak to Aaron and his sons, saying, 'This is the way you shall bless the children of Israel. Say to them:

"The LORD bless you and keep you; The LORD make His face shine upon you, And be gracious to you; The LORD

lift up His countenance upon you, And give you peace."'
"So they shall put My name on the children of Israel, and I
will bless them." (Numbers 6:22-27)

Let's consider three truths about the blessing.

1. It is a command of the Lord to the priests. If we
   are called to be the priests of our families, then I
   believe this blessing can be given to our wives and
   children through us.
2. It is to be spoken. God is a verbal God, and He
   speaks blessing over His people.
3. It is from the Lord, not us. Some people say, "I bless
   you," but Moses and Aaron were instructed to say,
   "The Lord bless you." And there's a reason for that:
   verse 27, *"So shall they put My name on them...and
   I will bless them"* (Emphasis added).

For the past ten years, every night, I have prayed a
blessing for my wife before we go to sleep. It's the last
thing I do before I lapse into unconsciousness. And God
has used that time to truly bless her and bless our marriage. It has also been my practice for those same years
to pray for my children before they go to bed. One by one

they will come to me before heading up the stairs, and I will lay a hand on their head or on their shoulder and ask the Lord to bless them and keep them. I may pray about something big going on in their lives or something important coming up the next day, but it is a time each day when I can make physical, as well as spiritual, contact with my children (who are not children any more, but are all adults, 12 years old or older!)

Remember the camping trip that ended up with a dead transmission? After the boys and I had played 36 holes of disc golf in the 98-degree heat that day, we had pizza and Coke and talked for a while in Caleb's apartment. I asked them, "Is there anything in your relationship with any one of your brothers, or with me, that needs to be addressed?" We went around the circle, and all five of them answered. As I had figured, there wasn't anything major going on, just a few minor hurts from past conflicts that had already been mended, but still were a bit tender around the edges. The question, though, gave each of them an opportunity to look their brothers and their dad in the eye and say, "There's no bad blood here. I am with you." It gave me an opportunity to look at my sons and say, "I love you five men and am proud of every one of you."

I would not trade anything for that weekend, just like I would not trade anything for any one of my five sons. I am a very rich man, indeed.

Part Three: Faithful Men as Protectors

Chapter 10
Are you not a man?!

S o far we have examined what the Scriptures say, in part, about men as prophets and men as priests. What is the primary job of the prophet? To hear from God. What is the prophet to do with what he has heard? Communicate it to God's people, in this case, to his family. The prophet is also called to disciple his children ("bring them up in the training") and to discipline his children ("and admonition of the Lord.") (Ephesians 6:4). The priest has two primary functions: to go before his children on behalf of God, and to go before God on behalf of his children. He fulfills the first function when he pursues a relationship with his children and walks them through sins and problems all the way to repentance. He fulfills the second function as he leads them as a worshiper, as an intercessor, and as someone who seeks wisdom from the Lord for them. Finally, the priests were commanded by God to put His name on the children of Israel as a blessing. Let's look now at the third footing, if you will, for a man's foundation as a leader: man as protector.

Men, God has put in us from birth a desire to protect. That is standard equipment for men. When a man is protecting his family, it is a picture that makes sense and fits with the reality of God's divine plan. When a woman is left to fend for herself, or she tries to assume the role as protector of her household, it is a pitiful sight, one that brings shame, one that makes us shake our heads in bewilderment and even disgust. There are two common movie plots that involve a man who is challenged in his protection of the family. In the first plot, the man wimps out, and his wife has to step up and do whatever it takes to protect the family. Woman triumphs; man is shamed. In the second plot, the man does whatever it takes, even taking the law into his own hands, to protect his family. Real men love the second plot. So-called "liberated women" love the first plot. But *men* are called to protect.

1 Samuel 26 records the story of David and Abishai sneaking into Saul's encampment one night while everyone was asleep, everyone including Abner, the commander of Saul's army and the one who was therefore

responsible to protect Saul. David could have speared Saul to death, but he knew that was not permitted by the Lord, so he just took Saul's spear and jug of water that were near his head. Then he ran to the top of a hill nearby and yelled like a wild man until everybody in Saul's camp woke up. David yelled, "Do you not answer, Abner?"

Abner cried, "Who *are* you, calling out to the king?" (1 Samuel 26:14)

I love David's response. He asks, "Are you not a man?" (Hey, Abner, are you a *man*?!) "And who *is* like you in Israel? Why then have you not guarded your lord the king? For one of the people came in to destroy [him]" (1 Samuel 26:15). David then goes on to say that Abner has messed up royally and deserves to die.

Let me ask you, and myself, "Are you not a man?" (1 Samuel 26:15) Who is like you in your household? Who is equipped by God like you are equipped by God? Are you guarding the treasure that has been entrusted to you? For you must *know* that the world and the devil are trying to come in and destroy that treasure.

One of my memories from childhood was one that I slept through, so I heard the story from my older brother and my parents. One night, a badly intoxicated man tried to bash in our front door around two a.m. My dad got his 12-gauge shotgun and stood guard just inside the front door, while Mom called the sheriff's department (This was in pre-911 days.). Mom paced nervously while the drunken man was ramming his body into our door. Dad sat calmly on the steps, gun ready, and I am quite confident he would have done whatever it took to protect his family. Two things about that story. Number one, it was one of the coolest things I slept through as a child, and I regret it to this day. I was a red-blooded kid who would have loved to see my dad standing guard, ready to fight for his family. The second thing about that story of my dad standing guard: what kind of older brother doesn't wake up his younger siblings (I think my baby brother slept through it, too) when something like this is going on?

Anyway, that memory always makes me think of Nehemiah. Remember when Nehemiah was rebuilding the walls in Jerusalem, and he was being threatened by Tobias and Sanballat and enemies who planned to come and attack? What did he do? He stationed the men to rebuild the wall in front of their own houses. If the wall was weak, it would compromise the safety of their families. He was a wise man and a great leader. Nehemiah knew that a healthy fear of attack on a man's own family would be a great motivator for him to build the wall well and not stop until it was done.

Men are called by God to protect, and this goes back to the garden. God created Adam first. He gave Adam His Word. "Of every tree of the garden you may freely eat; but of the tree of the knowledge of good and evil you shall not eat, for in the day that you eat of it you shall surely die" (Genesis 2:16-17). Eve was then created to be Adam's helpmeet, and it was clear that God held Adam responsible when he failed to protect Eve from deception. She took of the fruit and ate it, then gave some to Adam, whom, the Bible says was "with her" (3:6). The next thing you know, darkness had fallen on the earth forever, and God came calling, "Where are you?" (3:9) He could have just as easily said, "Adam, where *were* you?" Your wife was deceived, and you were standing right there watching! You were watching it happen and did nothing to stop it, nothing to protect her, nothing to protect your family, nothing to protect the generations that would come from your loins. Now look what has happened as a result. Men, nothing good can come from a man abdicating his responsibility to protect. Paul addresses this responsibility in 2 Corinthians 11:1-3.

Oh, that you would bear with me in a little folly—and indeed you do bear with me. For I am jealous for you with godly jealousy. For I have betrothed you to one husband, that I may present *you as* a chaste virgin to Christ. But I fear, lest somehow, as the serpent deceived Eve by his craftiness, so your minds may be corrupted from the simplicity that is in Christ.

Notice that Paul refers to the marriage covenant here as an analogy to the church. He is warning the church to listen to her husband, Christ, so she is not deceived like Eve was deceived. There is no question that our Husband will speak and has spoken clearly through His Word to protect us from every deception. But the potential for being deceived is always present and is a sure thing when we ignore our godly head. Men, you are the godly head of your household. We have established that, haven't we? Paul makes it clear in 1 Corinthians 11:3 that you are the head of your wife, just as Christ is your head, and God is the head of Christ. Exercise godly jealousy, then, over your household. In the same way, we are to pray for, establish, and hold onto with our very lives, a godly jealousy toward our wives and toward our children.

No one in his right mind would allow another man

to waltz through the front door of his house, take his wife by the hand and lead her away to do whatever he wanted. No one in his right mind would allow a stranger to come into his house and carry off one of his children. The truth is, however, that men allow that kind of kidnapping, that kind of deception, on a spiritual or emotional level, to take place much more often than we would be willing to admit. We allow false teachers to fill our family members' minds through TV, movies, or music which have content that does not honor Christ. We allow our children to spend time with people who are committed to a godless worldview and not shy about preaching their views to others. We are to exercise a godly jealousy for our wives and children spiritually and emotionally, just as we do physically. Paul then says, "I fear...as the serpent deceived Eve,... so your minds may be corrupted." There is a godly fear that motivates us to action.

Nahum sounded the alarm when he knew the enemy was coming to defeat Ninevah. This was one hundred years after the greatest revival ever, when a whole city had turned from sin to belief in Jehovah God. Now a century later, the city was apostate, and God was sending the Babylonians to destroy it. He spoke through His prophet

Nahum in chapter two, "He who scatters has come up before your face. Man the fort! Watch the road! Strengthen *your* flanks! Fortify *your* power mightily" (Nahum 2:1).

May I address you men who work with women? You are absolutely vulnerable to having an affair with every woman in your workplace. Period. I have promised Cindy that I would never have a secretary at Antioch who is female, unless it is one of my daughters or someone 70 years old or older, especially since I work at church alone with no other staff. Men, watch this. Like Alistair Begg says, your shoulders are reserved for only one woman to cry on. If you allow a woman in your office to start telling you her problems, your natural desire to protect women will well up, and the next thing you know, your marriage is in big trouble. "It would never happen to me; I can handle it," you say? Famous last words. Man the fort, men! Watch the road! I hear on a weekly basis of men in the ministry who have fallen prey to this temptation. I know that but for the grace of God, there go I, so I have placed some roadblocks up to help me man the fort. I will not counsel a woman alone in my office, for example. When a woman in the church wants to talk to me about a spiritual issue, I first ask her if she has talked to her own husband about it. He is her covering and her protector. If she has, and her husband has suggested that she talk to the pastor, then I try and schedule a meeting with both of them. If that is not possible, then I meet her with my wife present. I understand that some of you men have no choice about working with women in your office or company; it is simply an unavoidable reality. The point is that we always have a choice as to *how* we will conduct ourselves in the workplace, and how we will protect our marriage in the process.

Man the fort. We need to wake up to the fact that the one who scatters, the enemy of our souls, has come up before our face. He is on the doorstep, and we cannot slumber or sleep. There is an interesting picture on the cover of *Reforming Marriage* by Douglas Wilson (which is almost required reading for every man at Antioch Community Church). Entitled *The Sleeping Couple*, and painted by Jan Steen in the 1650's, it is a graphic picture of the condition of many of our households in the church in America. We sleep while the enemy plunders. We need to man the fort, watch the road leading to our household, and make repairs where the wall has already been breached.

Chapter 11
Building the hedge

So, let's address the questions. What do we need to protect our family from? How do we do it?

First, we protect our family from false doctrine. As we have seen in 2 Corinthians 11, Paul is warning the church against the deception that creeps in when we turn from the simplicity of the gospel. He warns in verse four of someone who comes preaching another Jesus, a different spirit, or a different gospel. He could have written this letter to the church of the 21st century. The "Jesus" of the prosperity gospel, the "spirit" of the modern pragmatism and church marketing movement, the "gospel" that is found in the message outside a local church that reads, "Jesus never rejected anyone...neither do we" all represent false doctrine.

How do we protect our family from false doctrine? By teaching true doctrine. We spent two years as a family working through the book, *Training Hearts Teaching*

Minds: Family Devotions based on the Shorter Catechism, by Starr Meade. The book provided a wonderful hedge for my children against false doctrine and taught them how to recognize it quickly. It is true that the greatest defense against counterfeits is an intimate knowledge of the real thing. Another book that served us well in this area of learning doctrine is *Total Truth* by Nancy Pearcey. We spent more than two years reading through it in the morning as an addition to our reading in the Scriptures. Many times the Lord used a section of the book to speak directly to a situation we were facing as a family or as a church. We are now reading through Pearcey's companion piece to *Total Truth,* entitled *Saving Leonardo.* Another excellent resource for training our families in a biblical worldview is *Dug Down Deep,* by Josh Harris.

I would also recommend dinnertime discussions as a way of building the hedge. I was at a wedding recently with my family, and the man officiating the ceremony said to the bride and groom, "You are making a promise to one another today that you will keep forever." I know he meant well, and certainly a marriage covenant is a promise before God, but I asked my children about it at our next meal. I wanted them to see the subtlety of the thinking that could lead a husband to make an idol out of his wife or vice versa. Or make an idol out of the marriage itself or the family. Our marriage covenant is temporal and only lasts as long as we both shall live, but our relationship with God is eternal and transcends all others.

Dinnertime often leads to discussions about the culture. As we pass the pasta salad, we will talk about movies we have seen or books we are reading. For example, we watched and talked about the movie, *Get Low,* starring Robert Duvall. I found the movie to be an excellent depiction of the futility of turning to asceticism as a way to atone for past sins. The lead character lives as a hermit nearly his whole adult life, never finding cleansing and forgiveness, never enjoying the fellowship and companionship of other people and the body of Christ. I will try to point out works-based religion also, when it is displayed either for good or for ill on the big screen. I recommend the 2003 movie, *Luther,* starring Joseph Fiennes. It paints a powerful picture of the corruption and the materialism of the 16th century Roman Catholic church, and it led to great discussions in our family about works-based religion. We talk about movies that tell a story of our nation's history and the good character and deeds, as well as the flaws, of the men and women who lived before us. *Gods and Generals* shows the genius of Robert E. Lee, as well as his pride. *Patton* paints a sad picture of the man who commanded the U.S. Third Army which made greater advances, captured more enemies, and liberated more territory in less time than any other army in history. Yet, this great commander had trouble controlling his own tongue and I would warn you about watching this movie without TV Guardian or some other profanity filter.

Dinnertime also leads to discussions about what the people around us are thinking and talking about. I will often share stories from the college public-speaking class I have taught for twenty years, and ask my children if they can think of biblical teaching that would apply to the situations that arise in the classroom. For example, I hear speeches every year about why abortion should be a woman's right because "it is her body and her choice," or why homosexual marriage is as valid as heterosexual marriage because "the issue is love, not gender." As we talk about this around the dinner table, I ask my children to explain why, from a biblical perspective, abortion and homosexuality are not acceptable in the eyes of God. When we have discussions like that, the goal is not to condemn the world but to exercise ourselves toward godliness, as Paul said in 1 Timothy 4:7. I want my children to "be wise as serpents and harmless as doves," as Jesus taught His disciples to be in Matthew 10:16. When we gather at the dinner table for such doctrinal discussions, I believe we are putting Deuteronomy 6 into practice as God tells us to "talk of them [His commands] when you sit in your house, when you walk by the way, when you lie down, and when you rise up" (6:7) You protect your family from false doctrine by teaching them correct doctrine. Most of the New Testament epistles are written, in part, to correct false doctrine and to teach correct doctrine. Just reading through a book like 1 Corinthians with your family for devotions, a few verses at a time, will introduce a number of doctrinal issues that must be addressed biblically if our children are to learn how to live for Christ.

You also protect your family by your own example. This goes back to the maxim that we tend to believe what we see more than what we hear. If your wife and children clearly see you walking in the truth, Dad, your obedience will build a hedge of protection around them higher and deeper than any other tool you have at your disposal. If they see you stumbling in the very things you rail against to them, and there is no remorse or repentance when you fall, they will learn by example that doctrine is to be studied and discussed, but practicing it is optional. The fruit will taste horrible, and the pain will last for many generations.

Protect your family from false doctrine.

Chapter 12
Touching their hearts

The second thing we need to protect our families from is bad companions. Proverbs 13:20 says, "He who walks with wise *men* will be wise, but the companion of fools will be destroyed." Do a study on fools in the Proverbs. There are five types, represented by five different Hebrew words. The *simple fool* is simple and needs instruction. He is foolish because he is ignorant. He opens his mind to any passing thought. The *silly fool* is one who is perverse in his speech and thinking. The silly fool resists instruction and needs punishment from authorities. The *sensual fool* is one who is committed to doing whatever brings him immediate pleasure. He is warned about more than any other type, as in the verse above where God tells us that the companion of this type of fool will be destroyed. The *mocking fool* is not willing to listen to rebuke. Proverbs 13:1 says, "A wise son *heeds* his father's instruction, but a scoffer does not listen to rebuke." The *committed fool* has rejected God and will lead others to do the same, if he can. Psalms 14:1 says, "The fool has said in his heart, '*There is* no God.' They are corrupt, they have done abominable works, there is none who does good.

All of our children are simple fools, at least when they are young and without the Spirit of God. Proverbs 22:15 tells us, "Foolishness *is* bound up in the heart of a child; the rod of correction will drive it far from him." Dads, we must do everything in our power to protect our children from ever becoming a silly, sensual, mocking, or committed fool. How do we do it?

To begin with, keep them from being companions with those four types of fools. You cannot possibly do this unless you know who your children's friends are and what their character is like. We can go from the sublime to the ridiculous here, I know. In every community there are parents who put their children in summer programs from 8 a.m. until 5 p.m. Sometimes the parents do that because they both work. Sometimes they do it simply because they don't want to be bothered, like one woman I heard about who spent her summer days at the local pool while her children were being supervised by strangers in a summer day camp. She did not know her children's guardians. I am sure that most of them were upstanding young men and women, but it is possible that one or more of them may have been predators. She did not know her children's companions. Though almost all of them were silly fools, standard-issue with kids, some of them were sensual fools, or worse. Sensual fools come in all ages and sizes, and often they are waiting for our children, and for us, to let our guards down. I have a friend whose son was molested in a local restaurant's men's room. He let his little boy go in to use the bathroom, and some terrible things happened. Was he a bad dad? No, he just let his guard down for a few moments, and his son suffered the consequences.

Second, to protect our children from becoming fools, make some difficult decisions that, though they may not be popular with your children, the rewards will far outweigh the complaints. Men, though we do not want to have a fortress mentality, nor do we ever have to make decisions based on fear, there *are* some common sense things we can do to protect our children. Here are a few that the Foxes do; feel free to disregard any or all of them.

1. We do not let our younger children play with their friends unless they are going to be supervised by

an adult that we trust. This of course is the ideal; we certainly let them play in the next room, or outside, with children of friends who are visiting our home.

2. We do not allow our children to go to sleepovers or slumber parties, no matter who the sleepover is with. We have made an exception to this rule for our older children, on rare occasions, or with their grandparents or with grown siblings in their homes.

3. We do not let our children see any movie unless we have approved it. Same with TV programs.

4.   We do not let our children read a book unless we have approved it. Same with magazines.

5. We talk to them, our daughters especially, about what to do if there is ever any danger, or if someone touches them inappropriately.

6. We keep the lines of communication open so that our children (and our young adults) know that they can come and talk. And we *ask* them to come and talk. Regularly.

Protect your children from becoming companions of fools. Take steps, even if they are difficult, to protect your children's hearts.

The third thing we need to protect our children from is from making a lifelong mistake. Listen up, young men. There is a mistake you can make that will literally haunt you for the rest of your life. Most of our mistakes are fixable with little consequence, like taking the wrong job, buying the wrong house, even going to the wrong church. *But there is nothing to be done for marrying the wrong wife.* At least, nothing that does not involve misery, torment, and heartache. So, the question is this: what is the greatest hedge against you marrying the wrong person, young man? I believe the answer is simple: the counsel of your father and your mother. Abraham sent his servant to get a wife for Isaac. I love this verse in Genesis 24:67, "Then Isaac brought her into his mother Sarah's tent; and he took Rebekah and she became his wife, and he loved her." He trusted the choice of his father's servant. Listen, men, I am not suggesting arranged marriages. But I do agree with Alistair Begg who says in his series of sermons entitled, "We Two Are One," and I paraphrase, "We raise young people who come to us for every decision. 'Does this tie match this shirt? Should I go to this party? Which college should I go to? What car should I buy?'

And then when it comes time for them to pick a mate for life, we shove them out the door to do it on their own. Or they just *go* out and pick someone and show up on the doorstep with, 'Hey, meet Jane. She's the girl I'm going to marry!' The biggest decision of a young person's life, and they are making it on their own!" (Begg's sermons are available at www.truthforlife.org)

No, we must be protectors. So, young men, listen to the counsel of your parents and resolve in your heart that you will never even entertain the thought of marrying without their blessing. Fathers, step up and step in and start leading in this area by learning about the principles of courtship, or Christian dating, if you prefer that model and believe it is the best one for your son or daughter. I can honestly say that the process Cindy and I walked through with Micah as he chose Kari to be his wife was one of the most blessed times of our 29-year marriage. We have never had a question as to whether she is the right one for him, and he would not have moved forward in the relationship without that knowledge. As I am writing this chapter, my second son is walking through courtship with a young lady, and he is doing it with his parents' blessing. I might add that he waited, sometimes even patiently(!), for that blessing for three years. I have spoken on the subject of courtship and how it has worked in our family. You can order a copy of the compact disc from me by going to www.antiochchurch.cc and sending me an order form for "Courtship: Does it Really Work?"

One final thing I will say about our job, men, as protectors. We are also called to protect our wives from carrying more than they can, or should, carry. Though it is not politically correct to say this any longer, it is still biblically correct and will be until the trumpet sounds: women are the weaker vessel. They are designed by God to be our helpers, not to be the primary load-bearer for the family. Peter instructed husbands to give honor to their wives, "as to the weaker vessel," and he even said that failure to do so would result in our prayers being hindered (1 Peter 3:7). We are charged by God to dwell with our wives according to understanding, and to learn how much our wives can and should handle. We must be attentive to their countenance and listen for the discouragement that can creep in when they feel like they are *not* "all in this together." This will be covered more thoroughly in the next section, but it begins with communication. We help our wives learn to tell us the whole truth about how they are feeling and how they are doing, and *we learn* how to hear that as honest communication and not as complaining. I can say from much experience that when my wife is feeling overwhelmed and shares something of that with me, and I react with defensiveness or accusation or anything other than tender kindness, the results are not pleasant.

Wedding invitations sometimes say, "Today I am marrying my best friend." I married my best friend nearly 30 years ago. The world has changed a lot since then, but several things are still the same. The ocean is still crashing on the shore. The church is still alive and strong. Gravity is still working; I fell hard for Cindy then, and I am falling in love with her more and more every day. Cindy is still my best friend, and we are more committed to loving each other to the very end than we ever dreamed of in our twenties. I thank God for that, and pray that He will never let me take it for granted, and that my heart will always be to man the fort, to watch the road, to strengthen the flanks. My family is worth it.

Men, we are called by God to protect. It's our job. Square those shoulders, swell up that chest, and do it proudly.

Part Four: Faithful Men as Providers

Chapter 13
Improving your vision

S o far in this series of challenges, we have seen that men are called to be prophets in their homes. That means they are responsible to hear from God, communicate what they hear to their families, disciple their children and their wives, and discipline their sons and daughters. Second, we saw that men are called to be priests in their homes, to go before their families on behalf of God and to go before God on behalf of their families. Third, we saw that God has put into the heart of every man to be the protector of his home. We are to protect our families from false doctrine, bad companions, wrong marriages. We also must protect the emotions of our wives; they can be deceived, and they can also be overwhelmed by carrying loads they are not supposed to carry.

There is another responsibility that God has given us as men: to be the providers in our homes.

Now when you think of being the provider, it may be that your mind goes first to 1 Timothy 5:8. "But if anyone does not provide for his own, and especially for those of his household, he has denied the faith and is worse than an unbeliever."

This is the classic verse many think of when we talk about a man's responsibility to provide for his household. The context of the verse has to do with providing for our widowed mothers, so it stands to reason that we are also called to provide for our wives and children. This has been true since the Garden of Eden. God gave Adam a job before He gave him a wife. But is that all there is to being a provider? Has the man who brings home enough money every week to pay the bills fulfilled his responsibility as a provider? No, I don't think so. In fact, the word used in 1 Timothy 5:8 for provide literally means "to take thought, to care beforehand." It can also mean "to perceive before, to foresee." It suggests that the provider thinks about those for whom he is responsible, perceives what their needs are, and makes provision for them ahead of time, as much as he is able. This certainly includes provision for physical needs, but it goes much deeper than that, which we will explore in a moment. Where do we look to learn about being a provider? We look to God, our heavenly Father, who is a perfect provider. God has freely given us the example we are to follow.

When Isaac was walking up Mount Moriah with his father Abraham, carrying the wood for the offering while his father carried the fire and the knife, Isaac asked, "Where *is* the lamb for a burnt offering?" Abraham's famous reply was, "My son, God will provide for Himself the lamb for a burnt offering." (Genesis 22:7-8) God did provide the sacrifice to take Isaac's place, and we can clearly see that this provision had nothing to do with a power bill or groceries or a comfortable place to sleep. God's provision for Abraham that day was spiritual. God provided a sacrifice to take Isaac's place, just as Jesus, the perfect lamb of God, would one day take your place and mine. God's provision for Elijah when he was running from Jezebel was spiritual as well; He encouraged the fiery prophet that he was not the only faithful follower of God in all of Israel. But God also provided for Elijah's physical needs: He gave him sleep and food.

God will provide. He provided food for His children in the wilderness, manna, and He gave them shoes that did not wear out. He led them by day with a cloud and by night with a pillar of fire. God provided protection for them when they had to conquer the Promised Land. He provided houses for His people to live in and vineyards for them to eat from, vineyards which they had not planted. And on it goes, until in the New Testament Jesus said that our heavenly Father who takes care of the sparrow and the lily will also take care of us, and much more.

God is the provider for every household. Even when a man has a good job that produces enough income to pay a tithe, pay the bills, *and* pay the savings account, that man should never say, "*I* provide for my family." No, God provides for your family, and for mine, through the means of grace He has chosen, whether that means of grace is a job or a raven carrying a morsel of food or a ram caught in a thicket. God is the provider. God is the giver, and He delights in it. He delights in being the One to whom we owe all of our praise and thanksgiving. He delights in giving freely to His children and blessing them beyond measure. But God knows the tendency of man's heart to be proud and to think that what he has earned by the sweat of his brow has been independent, somehow, from God's grace and God's enabling. He reminded the children of Israel of this in the wilderness when He said,

"And you shall remember the Lord your God, for *it is* He who gives you power to get wealth, that He may establish His covenant which he swore to your fathers, as *it is* this day" (Deuteronomy 8:18).

God provides. He teaches us to do the same. He has called and equipped us to provide for our families. What then does a man provide? *First, he provides a vision for his family.*

Vision casting is a powerful tool in your toolbox, Dad.

In a commencement speech delivered to his alma mater, Ohio Wesleyan, in 2006, Byron Pitts communicated: "A newspaper reporter interviewed my mom for a story about me and asked, 'Mrs. Pitts, how did you manage as a single parent, a divorcee, to send three kids to college?' Her answer: 'It was simple. I said, Go to college, or I will beat you to death.'"

Pitts is a contributor to *60 Minutes* and chief national correspondent on the *CBS Evening News*. How did a man who could not read at the age of twelve reach the pinnacle of success in his field? He tells that story in his book, *Step Out on Nothing*, and if I had to summarize the book, I would say that Byron Pitts overcame many hardships through the help of a loving God who gave him faith to believe, a mother who would not take no for an answer, and a few mentors who saw more than just a boy who stuttered or a young man who was slow in his studies. He gives them credit in a chapter entitled, "The Hands that Pull You Up," which opens with a quote by his grandmother, Roberta Mae Walden, "You can't climb a mountain without some rough spots to hold onto"(p. 81).

Pitts was ready to drop out of college as a freshman after his English professor expressed, "Your presence at Ohio Wesleyan University is a waste of my time and the government's money. I think you should leave" (pp. 105-106). He walked over to the administration building, crushed by his professor's words, and picked up the papers necessary for withdrawal. Sitting on a bench outside, and with tears running down his cheeks, Pitts filled out the papers. It was at that moment that his life changed. A woman walked by, and seeing his tears, asked if he was OK. He explained the situation, and she said, "Now give me your word you will speak to me tomorrow before you make any final decision on school! Give me your word! Look me in the eye and give me your word!"(p. 116). Her name was Ulle Lewes, and as Pitts describes, "If ever I doubted that angels really do exist, those doubts were now cast aside" (p. 117). He agreed to meet with her, and the next day she began to cast a vision for success in Byron Pitts' life, meeting with him every week for three to four hours at a time.

I am reminded of people who spoke into my life, who cast a vision for me, who said in as many words, "I believe in you. More than that, I believe God can use you. Don't quit." I had a college professor at UNC who taught me in my first speech class how to take a piece of literature and understand it better through performing it. Sometime during the course of that semester, Prof. Hardy pulled me aside and said, "Mark, why aren't you a speech communications major?" I stammered and sputtered until she said, "You should be. You're good at it." I have looked back many times to that pivotal point in my life and how God directed me through a professor who cast a vision for success. God directed me into ministry through a pastor and a missions director. Stephen Crotts saw potential in me for ministry and asked me to start a coffeehouse for young people in 1983. "His Place" became a hangout for teens and young adults who were looking for something to do on Saturday nights, and it provided a place where Cindy and I could meet them and minister to their needs. J.L. Williams watched that happening for a while and then asked me to lead the musical team called "New Directions" in the summers of 1984-1986. It was in those years that I began to preach regularly, after the group had done a concert, and God lit a fire in my bones to preach and later to help plant a church. These two men saw something in me and encouraged me in it.

I think it is one of our most important missions as parents: to see the good in our children, or what God has put there, and encourage them in it. We are sometimes so busy trying to correct what is wrong (and there's plenty of that to go around, in us *and* in them) that we miss the bigger picture. Let's not miss those golden moments of opportunity to cast a vision for our children and for others with whom the Lord will give us influence. Our words of blessing can be used by God to change someone's life. I will tell you that my greatest ally in all of this has been my wife. She has been the discerning one most of the time, who has seen something in one of our children that God put there for His glory. She will tell me about it, and that gives me the help I need to start looking for it myself, and then to talk with my son or daughter. Listen to your wives on this, men! Ask them to help you see what your children's bents are, where they have strong gifts or talents that can be developed and used for God's glory.

I have had the privilege to teach all of my children in the writing classes that I offer for local teenagers. All of my children have done well with writing, and we encourage them to use that gift for the Lord. Two years ago, our daughter Hannah began to adapt the book *The Last Sin Eater*, by Francine Rivers, for the stage. She got permission to produce it, and it made it to the stage for the first time ever in July 2011. The script was excellently written, and the show was used by God to encourage believers and challenge unbelievers with the claims of the gospel. The Bible says, "For we are His workmanship, created in Christ Jesus for good works, which God prepared beforehand that we should walk in them" (Ephesians 2:10).

You are the visionary for your household, Dad. That means, first of all, that you have been given a purpose for your own life and ministry. You have been given a large vision, a God-sized purpose to fulfill in His name and for His glory. How do I know that? I know it mainly because of what God's Word says! He gives all His sons and daughters a purpose and a calling. There is not a random molecule in the universe. Neither is there a man or woman, boy or girl, called by His name and created in His image that does not have value and purpose before God. "He chose us in Him before the foundation of the world, that we should be holy and without blame before Him in love, having predestined us to adoption as sons by Jesus Christ to Himself, according to the good pleasure of His will, to the praise of the glory of His grace" (Ephesians 1:4-6).

I know this is true for you married men for another reason. The very fact that God has brought a helpmate to you is proof that you have a God-sized purpose to fulfill that you cannot accomplish alone. So, the question is, what is your purpose? What is your calling? What has God set you down on the earth to do? If you don't know, that would be the most important discovery of your life up until now, apart from your salvation by grace and through faith. Don't just exist. Don't just try and make it safely to your deathbed. *Find* the purpose for which you were created and *live* it! If you are married, this is a large part of the purpose of God for you: to lay down your life for your bride as Jesus did for His. If you have children, this is a large part of the purpose of God for you: to train up your children in the instruction and admonition of the Lord. If you have a job, then this is a part of your purpose and calling: to do all to the glory of God. God can use any vocation, as long as it does not call us to compromise the truth of God's Word, to bring glory and honor to Him.

When John Newton was the captain of a slave ship, there is no question in my mind that he was not serving God in the vocation that God chose for him from before the foundation of the earth. There are vocations to avoid, and sailing a slave ship would be one of them. There are jobs that add greatly to your bank account while they steal from your soul and rob you of the joy of your salvation and the peace of God. Find another as quickly as you can and walk away from that job or career that is crushing your life. Or in some cases, like working in an abortion clinic, I would say walk away first, and trust God will help you find another way to make a living. What if you have a job that does not require you to sin, at least not overtly, but the job itself demands 18-hour days, and you have no time for your wife and children? My answer to men who live that way is simple: you are giving the leftovers to your family and your church. Find another job that will not require that of you.

You are a visionary, Dad, who has been given a purpose from God for your life. That purpose is greater than a vocation, but certainly includes it. That purpose cannot be described as anything less than to display the glory of God before your family by becoming like Him. Peter Schemm, Jr. says, "It should be the lifelong pursuit of all earthly fathers to imitate God the Father...I want to mediate fatherhood in a way that attracts my wife and children to the gospel—and to the great architect of the gospel, God the Father, the one from whom every family in heaven and on earth are named" (*The Journal of Family Ministry, Vol. 1.2, p. 65*).

That's a God-sized vision, Dad. Your wife is given to be your helpmeet to accomplish that vision. Your children have also been given to share in your vision while they are young and to be trained to walk out their own vision and purpose as they grow up and prepare to leave home.

What is your vision for your family? What do you want to accomplish more than anything else with your children before you let them go towards their own purpose, those children who are "arrows in the hand of a warrior?" (Psalm 127:4). A warrior has a target for every arrow; he lets none fly without taking careful aim, they are so precious. So we should do like the prophet suggested and "write the vision and make it plain" (Habakkuk 2:2). Here are the purposes that I have for my own children:

First, that each has a vibrant and growing relationship with Jesus Christ and a love for His Word and His church. We cannot make that happen, but we can certainly pray for it and help facilitate it.

Second, that each has solid, biblical character.

Third, that each is a servant with a solid work ethic.

Fourth, that each learns to communicate with clarity and with passion.

Fifth, that each loves the gospel and holds fast to a biblical worldview.

That's where it starts. Write the vision, make it plain. Cindy and I wrote those five purposes down many years ago and then worked out various means of helping our children to accomplish each one. This is something you should revisit on a regular basis, at least once a year. Cindy and I try to have some kind of a quarterly retreat, where we go away for a night (or two) and enjoy time alone as a couple. At least one of those trips includes a session of making, assessing, and tweaking goals for our family, our marriage, and our children.

Following is the vision I have for our marriage:

First, that we will grow in love for one another for

God's glory, thereby increasing our reflection of Christ's relationship with His bride, the church.

Second, that we will grow in "like" with each other, thankful that we are best friends, and working to grow and protect that friendship.

Third, that Cindy and I will grow in our role as disciplers and encouragers of the next generation of leaders coming along, both here and in other places, as the Lord leads.

So, what would you say your vision for your family is? Have you ever sat down and written it out? I have heard Dave Ramsey encourage us many times to do this with our budget, with our financial goals and dreams. Isn't it even more important to do the same with our most precious "commodities"?

"*Where there is no vision* (emphasis added), the people cast off restraint" (Prov. 29:18).

A dad's job, then, is to provide a vision for his family. But not only that...

Chapter 14
Holding their hearts

Second, a man should provide for his family's emotional needs.

How many of us grew up in homes where there was good or even excellent financial provision, but we were starved for affirmation, for approval, for our father's love? Tom Eldredge wrote in his book, *Safely Home*:

Fathers must heed God's call, and begin to rebuild God's institution, the family...A man's decision to turn his heart to his family may cost him much of his spare time. It may require him to give up his hobbies. It may even force him to change his occupation. These things a man cannot take with him into the next life. But he can take his family. His decision will be rewarded in heaven. (pp. 85-87)

Consider the story of Jacob in Genesis. He was an excellent businessman: shrewd, savvy, capable. He amassed a great deal of wealth, and his children lived a very comfortable lifestyle, at least until the worldwide famine. But what kind of emotional support did he give his children? Not much—unless that child's name happened to be Joseph! Jacob played favorites, and his other ten sons (This was before Benjamin came along.) got more and more jealous, simply because they had an emotional need for their father's love and approval that was not being met. We know what happened. They sold their brother into slavery. They removed the object of their father's affection. What can happen to a child who is not given what he longs for most, his father's approval and love?

Gene Edward Veith writes in *World* magazine, "One factor in the development of male homosexuality, according to Christian psychologists, is the absence of a father figure. The boy so yearns for a father's love that he becomes attracted to men. The effect of absent or emotionally distant fathers on daughters is that they so yearn for a father's love that they often become promiscuous" (www.worldmag.com/articles/13473).

In *The Journal of Family Ministry*, Ken Canfield records the following:

Today, it's strikingly clear that fatherlessness and its negative outcomes impact all children, irrespective of ethnicity. The current and conservative cost of fatherlessness is estimated at one hundred billion dollars annually. Though a significant sum, money cannot account for the staggering emotional and moral costs, as well as 'loss of potential,' that plague a child disconnected from his or her dad. Currently in America, at least twenty-five million children under the age of 18 don't live with their natural father. Add the number of children who live with their fathers, but aren't connected emotionally, psychologically, or spiritually, and you have the dramatic majority of all children (*The Journal of Family Ministry, Vol. 1.2, p. 26*).

I remember vividly the comments that Bill Glass made many years ago when I heard him speak at an International Fellowship of Christian Businessmen's luncheon in Burlington, NC. Glass was a consensus All-American football player at Baylor University and a member of the 1964 Cleveland Browns who beat the Baltimore Colts to win the NFL World Championship two years prior to the first Super Bowl. After retiring from football, Glass traveled the world to preach the gospel and is perhaps best known for his prison ministry. He has preached to inmates in prisons all over the country and around the world, and the day I heard him at a luncheon, he said, "There may be a man in prison somewhere who doesn't hate his father—I have just never met him." He told the story of the greeting card company that offered free Mother's Day cards to violent criminals incarcerated in a maximum security prison. Thousands of the men accepted the offer and sent a card to their mothers. The greeting card company, buoyed by their success, made the same offer for Father's Day. Glass said, "Not one inmate accepted the offer. Not one man sent his father a card for Father's Day." Are there negative consequences in a home where Dad is not involved and engaged emotionally with his children? Oh, yes.

What about the positive effects of a father in the home who is loving his children? Again, Ken Canfield informs us:

Infants who have time alone with their dad show richer social and exploratory behavior than do children not exposed to such experiences. They smile more frequently, in general, and they more frequently engage in playful behaviors with their dad. Children who sense closeness to their fathers are twice as likely to enter college or find stable employment after high school; they are seventy-five percent less likely to have a child in their teenage years, eighty percent less likely to spend time in jail, and half as likely to experience depression (*JFM*, Vol 1.2, p. 27).

There is simply no substitute for a dad who is blessing his children by providing for their emotional needs. This must be true of his love for his wife as well.

Consider Jacob, again. If we all agree that Jacob was not exactly a model father, we would probably agree that he wasn't exactly a model husband, either—at least with his first wife, Leah.

Look at Genesis 29: 30-35 for one of the saddest portions of Scripture related to marriage in the Bible:

Then *Jacob* also went in to Rachel, and he also loved Rachel more than Leah. And he served with Laban still another seven years. When the LORD saw that Leah was unloved, He opened her womb; but Rachel was barren. So Leah conceived and bore a son, and she called his name Reuben; for she said, "The LORD has surely looked on my affliction. Now therefore, my husband will love me." Then she conceived again and bore a son, and said, "Because the LORD has heard that I *am* unloved, He has therefore given me *this* son also." And she called his name Simeon. She conceived again and bore a son, and said, "Now this time my husband will become attached to me, because I have borne him three sons." Therefore his name was called Levi. And she conceived again and bore a son, and said, "Now I will praise the LORD." Therefore she called his name Judah. Then she stopped bearing.

Leah wanted desperately for her husband to love her. She kept giving him sons, perhaps thinking each time, "Now the Lord's blessing will provoke Jacob to love me." Each birth began with excitement and ended with disappointment. Leah tried four times, and Jacob still did not wake up to see the needs of his wife and love her as she needed him to love her. To Leah's great credit, and to God's praise, she did not allow her heart to become bitter. After Judah's birth, she stated, "Now I will praise the Lord"(Genesis 29:35). I believe she was saying, "God is my portion and my strength. I will delight myself in Him." There is an important truth in that: ultimately, no husband can fully meet his wife's emotional needs, and no wife can fully meet her husband's emotional needs; only God can do that for each one. But the story of Leah is sad because it *was* Jacob's responsibility to love his wife, even though she was not the only one. (Which, by the way, is a great argument for the teaching of Scripture that a man should have only one wife. Let's face it, men, it is a full-time job for each of us to love the *one* that God has given us!) Peter said to us, "Husbands...dwell with them with understanding" (1 Peter 3:7). We have been given the delightful task of getting to know our wives: studying them to learn what makes them happy, what makes them feel loved and appreciated, and what makes them feel protected and provided for. That's our job! I read a great little book a few years ago called *For Men Only* by Shaunti and Jeff Feldham. It helped me understand my wife's emotional needs better. I also recommend *This Momentary Marriage* by John Piper. Cindy and I have spent some time reading through that out loud together and have been blessed by it.

How can you make your wife feel loved? Every wife is different, and there is much to be said about discovering what your wife's "love language" is. But the truth is, all women feel loved when their husband praises them and is genuinely grateful for them. I have the opportunity to write a weekly newspaper column, which you know because you have already had to read through, or skip over, one of them in this book. When my wife turned fifty, I wrote a column entitled "Fifty Reasons Why I Love Her." It provoked many more positive responses than all of the columns I have written in the past seven years. The only response that mattered to me, though, was from Cindy.

I presented it to her on her birthday, as we were sitting down as a family to have breakfast together. It was a Saturday, the day that my column is in the paper. I cut it out and handed it to her. "Happy birthday, Darling," I said. She read it and began to weep:

Here are fifty reasons why I love my best friend, Cindy, who turns fifty today. You can count them if you like, but trust me, there are fifty. The verse fragments that are mixed in come from 1 Corinthians 13, the J. B. Phillips translation. Here are the nifty fifty, in no certain order.

She is beautiful. In fact, Cindy is the best looking fifty-year-old I know. She has a great sense of humor, evidenced by the fact that she laughs at my jokes. Many people don't (have a great sense of humor). She loves our children. Cindy is a great grandmother...or, a grandmother who is great. She cares for needs in the church. Not easily offended, she looks for ways to overlook it when others do her wrong. Cindy sings or hums when she is happy, and sometimes when she is not. She went to Carolina, and though she doesn't care about the teams like I do, she still cares... some. A little. Cindy helps me with my columns (except this one; this one is a surprise) and with my sermons. She is a great listener. She is able to give tough love when needed. Cindy reads voraciously, but eats carefully, and is intentional to make sure her family eats healthy, too. She loves good music, loves Holden Beach, and loves to go on long walks with me. Cindy does not notice when others do her wrong. She is slow to lose patience.

Cindy will cry during sad movies and laugh out loud until it hurts during funny ones. She is particular about keeping a clean house...but this does not paralyze her from having people over for a meal and good fellowship around the table. Cindy goes on a weekly date with me. She also has good friends she loves and keeps up with. She has a great alto voice and harmonizes beside me every Sunday in church. She has overcome her fear of public speaking, though it would not be in her top fifty things to do on her fiftieth. Cindy is faithful to pray when someone asks for it, and she does not keep an account of evil. She shares the joy of those who live by the truth.

Cindy is shorter than I am, which comes in handy on the rare occasion when we slow dance at wedding receptions. She likes to drink coffee with me in the evening, decaf, and enjoys a trip to the plethora of frozen yogurt places now available in Burlington. Cindy keeps a clean house, and a clean heart. She reads her Bible faithfully and lives by what she learns there every day. Cindy has a heart to give to those in need and is willing to go overseas on mission trips with me. She looks forward to the slower pace in the summer, and enjoys picking fresh fruit with her children, daughter-in-law and grandchildren at local farms. Cindy is not anxious to impress, nor does she cherish inflated ideas of her own importance.

Cindy runs three times a week to stay in shape and is planning to run her first 5K this fall. She has been the primary teacher of our children for twenty-three years. Cindy stands by me even when others might be looking for places to hide. She loves to worship and loves Jesus more than anyone or anything.

Cindy is my best friend, and after all these years, she is still my baby girl. Happy birthday, Darling.

I do, with all my heart, rejoice in the wife of my youth!

~~~

As they say, even a blind hog finds an acorn every now and then. I do not share this column with you to pat myself on the back, but to say to you men, *there is not a wife on earth who would respond to an effort like this with a roll of the eyes or an indifferent shrug.* Tell her that you love her and take the time to tell her why. She will respond. I promise.

Since that column was published in the newspaper, I have had a number of men tell me that it provoked them to write something for their wives. One pastor told me recently that his wife's birthday was coming up in about three weeks; "I am going to write something about her like that column where you shared those fifty reasons."

A man provides for the emotional needs of his family. And...

He provides for their financial needs.

There is no question that the biblical teaching is clear. God created Adam, put him in the garden, and told him to tend it and keep it. He gave him a job. Then God created Eve, put her next to her husband, and told Adam that she was his helpmate. Adam was oriented toward his calling. Eve was oriented toward her husband. Therein lies the problem and the design at the same time. Man is not oriented toward his wife; his primary focus, what wakes him up at night and what gets him excited during the day, is his calling, his vocation (which comes from the Latin "vocare," meaning to call). If a man tries to violate that God-given design and *not* work, either his wife will not be provided for, *or* she will have to provide for her household and take over his responsibility. Either scenario is a shame.

If a man works hard to provide for his family, he is to be praised, and should get the respect of his wife and his children. If he is not making enough money for his family to survive, he needs to work harder, take a second job, or even get more training or education to provide for his family. That's his responsibility. The challenge for many of us is balancing our two responsibilities: to work and provide an income for our families and to work and provide for their other needs, to the best of our ability.

I recommend Dave Ramsey's material in his *Financial Peace University* course as a tool to help you learn to manage the resources which God has provided. Cindy and I were blessed early in our marriage to be able to go through a similar program taught by Christian financial counselor Larry Burkett. We learned what stewardship meant for us as followers of Jesus Christ, and that we had a responsibility to earn, to give, to spend, and to save money. Learning how to keep those four in balance is a key to a healthier and happier marriage. All of our fights have not been money fights, by any means. But many of them have. The teaching of Dave Ramsey and others like him will give you the tools you need to be able to manage your money wisely and biblically.

A man provides for the financial needs of his family. And...

He provides for their spiritual needs.

We have covered most of this in previous sections of the book. A man who fulfills his role as a prophet and priest in his home will certainly be leading and feeding the flock God has entrusted to him. We neglect those responsibilities at our peril. Dads, we are those whom God has charged with the privilege and the responsibility to be the spiritual leaders of our homes. We cannot delegate that to our wives without paying a severe price down the road.

I think of David when Absalom killed Amnon for violating his sister. Absalom fled Jerusalem, remaining gone for three years, and the Bible says David "longed to go to [him]" (2 Samuel 13:39). Well, why didn't he? What Absalom needed right then was a father who would minister to his son and help him get clear in his heart with God. But David remained in Jerusalem. Then when Absalom did return to Jerusalem, with David's permission, David asserted, "Let him return to his own house, but do not let him see my face" (2 Samuel 14:24). Why? To save face? To make sure he looked "king-like"? I am not sure why David stayed away, but Absalom lived in Jerusalem for two whole years before he ever saw his father. By that time, it was too late. The seeds of rebellion, fertilized by bitterness and unforgiveness, led to a war and ultimately to Absalom's death (2 Samuel 13-14).

Will we provide for our children's spiritual needs, even at the cost of our own reputation, even if it means we have to run down that long road to embrace them, even if that child has shamed us and shamed the family?

A man provides for the spiritual needs of his family. Finally...

Chapter 15
Numbering our days

H e provides for his family's future.

I want to make sure that if I die today my wife will not have to go to work to provide for the family and will be able to keep homeschooling and to live in the same house. That's why I have a term life insurance policy that is worth around ten times what my family would need to live on. The idea is that Cindy could invest that amount and live off ten percent per year. There are lots of ways of doing that, and I am by no means a financial or estate planner. I recommend you get good advice through Dave Ramsey's website or through one of his ELPs, Endorsed Local Providers. To be honest, this is an area of our ministry as dads where we often fail, simply because we neglect to *take thought, to provide beforehand,* as Paul mentions in 1 Timothy 5:8.

Do you have a will? Nearly sixty percent of Americans don't, according to a 2008 survey by FindLaw.com. Without a written will, adults have little influence over what will happen to their assets and minor children after they die. (www.west.thompson.com) You can have a lawyer draft a will for you for about $500, or you can do it yourself through one of the many online sites that provide legal documents, like LegalZoom.com. I also recommend a Living Will. Legal Zoom's website explains, "A living will lets you specify decisions about artificial life support in advance. It not only ensures your wishes will be heard, but also protects your loved ones from having to make these difficult, deeply personal choices for you." (www.legalzoom.com) You may also want to consider drafting a Health Care Power of Attorney. It "grants your agent authority to make medical decisions for you if you are unconscious, mentally incompetent, or otherwise unable to make decisions on your own. While not the same thing as a living will, many states allow you to include your preference about being kept on life support. Some states will allow you to combine parts of the health care POA and living will into an advanced health care directive." (www.legalzoom.com)

Do you have a safe place where, in the event of your death, your wife can find what she needs to know about insurance, the mortgage, taxes, mutual funds, and more?

It is a good idea to have important papers in a fire-safe box in your home or in a safety deposit box at the bank. That box will include the titles to your vehicles, the deed to your land, your mortgage papers, birth certificates, social security cards, passports, and other important documents that you don't want to lose. I have also prepared a folder for Cindy entitled "Important Information." That document is on our computers, but there is a hard copy in the fire-safe box that I update every year or so, as needed. In that folder my wife (or my children, in the unlikely event that Cindy and I die together) can find information they need to help them move forward. Here are the categories I have included in that folder:

Life Insurance: who carries the coverage, how the premiums are paid, who to contact

Health Insurance: information on how to contact Samaritan Ministries (the medical sharing group we are a part of)

Homeowners Insurance: who carries the coverage, when the annual premium is due, who to contact

Car Insurance: who carries the coverage, how the premiums are paid, who to contact

Disability Insurance: who carries the coverage, how

the premiums are paid, who to contact

Mutual Funds: where they are located, how to contact, how the money is divided in the event of death

Social Security: numbers and cards for each member of the family

Last Will and Testament: a copy is in the fire-safe box and on file with the attorney, whose contact information is included

Deed to Land: a copy is in the fire-safe and on file with the attorney, whose contact information is included

Car Titles

Birth Certificates, Marriage License, Vaccination records

Passports

I also included a file in the folder entitled, "Who To Call When You Need …" It includes information with regard to:

Car Repair

Tires

Septic Service (who to call, frequency of service, next service due)

Plumbing

Electrical

Heating Fuel

HVAC (heating or AC unit) repair

Lawnmower Repair

Tax Preparation

Another way I try to provide for my family's future is by attempting to live as long as I possibly can! God is sovereign, and He numbered my days and fashioned them for me before even one of them came to be (Psalm 139:16), but that does not absolve me from my responsibility to take care of this old tent. If I am not taking care of my body, I am violating God's Word in at least a couple of ways. First, the Bible says that you are not your own, "For you were bought at a price; therefore glorify God in your body and in your spirit, which are God's" (1 Corinthians 6:20). The Bible also says, "For you are the temple of the living God" (2 Corinthians 6:16). Finally, we are told, "For bodily exercise profits a little, but godliness is profitable for all things, having promise of the life that now is and of that which is to come" (1 Timothy 4:8). I would say the Bible makes a strong case for temple maintenance. Keeping my body in shape includes eating right, exercising, going to the doctor for regular physicals, and keeping short accounts with people so that a root of bitterness does not spring up and defile many.

I am absolutely convinced that there is a connection between my physical discipline and my spiritual discipline. I would make the case that Paul states this in part when he says, "But I discipline my body and bring *it* into subjection, lest, when I have preached to others, I myself should become disqualified" (1 Corinthians 9:27). I remember looking for a church when I was a college student and hearing that a certain preacher at a certain church was a good expositor of the Word. I went and heard him, and it was true, he was an effective communicator of truth. But I had a hard time believing him. I knew I would not be coming back for a second visit, and it was simply because I felt like the way he treated his body disqualified him. He was well over 300 pounds, and as I was talking with people in the churchyard after the service, the preacher was doing that too, while he enjoyed a smoke. Maybe I judged the man unfairly, but I could not listen to someone telling me to deny myself and follow Christ while it was clear, at least from the outward appearance, that this man had a difficult time denying himself. Read *The Reformed Pastor,* especially if you are an elder or hold some position of spiritual leadership in the lives of others. Here is an appropriate excerpt:

Take heed to yourselves, because there are many eyes upon you, and there will be many to observe your falls. You cannot miscarry but the world will ring of it. The eclipses of the sun by day are seldom without witnesses. As you take yourselves for the lights of the churches, you may expect that men's eyes will be upon you. If other men may sin without observation, so cannot you. And you should thankfully consider how great a mercy this is, that you have so many eyes to watch over you, and so many ready to tell you of your faults; and thus have greater helps than others, at least for restraining you from sin. Though they may do it with a malicious mind, yet you have the advantage of it. God forbid that we should prove so impudent as to do evil in the public view of all, and to sin willfully while the world is gazing on us! (Richard Baxter, www. reformed.org/books/baxter/reformed_pastor)

I was at the YMCA a few years ago getting dressed to go work out. There was a man next to me on the bench getting undressed after his workout. He weighed at least 300 pounds and was probably pushing 400. The bench he sat on groaned and swayed under his girth, and I marveled at how long it took him just to bend over and untie his shoes and take them off. The sweat was pouring off him just from *that* exertion. But what I believe the Lord spoke to me that day was this, "At least he's taking a step. That's more than most men are doing these days. He has a hard road ahead, but he's on the way."

How about you, men? Are you on the way? Are you on the way to being the prophet, priest, protector and provider that God has called you to be? He is the One who equips us to lead. He is faithful.

Conclusion

Picture three grown sons standing around their father's bed on Christmas Day 2005. The four men of the family were together for the first time in at least fifteen years. The oldest grew up like many firstborns, wanting to please his dad, working for the company that gave his father a career, being a responsible son. The second son ran off to college, met his wife, and settled 75 miles away from his hometown. His relationship with his father had been strained over the years, sometimes because of his stubbornness and pride, sometimes because of his father's. The third son ran off to the beach after some run-ins with the law, and there he had stayed, without a driver's license but with a job, a moped, and a faithful dog. He too had a strained relationship with his father, whose feelings about his third son's lifestyle seemed to alternate between guilt and frustration.

Here they stood, all together again, brought to this place because their father was dying. He had been diagnosed three months earlier with cancer, and was doing all that he could to beat the disease. But the prognosis wasn't good, and the weight of their father's impending death muted the sons' laughter and rough teasing. They didn't know what to say. They listened to their father speak about growing up as one of eight children in a house where there were no extras and often not enough love to go around. "The only thing my parents ever gave me," he said, "was a .22 rifle." He went over the finances with his three sons, and began to cry as he spoke of leaving his wife, their mother, behind.

He said that he had not done a good job when the three boys were growing up of expressing how proud he was of them. "I couldn't have asked for three finer sons," he said. "I just wish I had done a better job giving encouragement and guidance for you three, but when I was growing up, all I got from my dad was the belt...and I guess I passed some of that on." The middle son responded, "Dad, we deserved every lickin' we got—and plenty we didn't get!" The father smiled tiredly and praised his two older sons for the way they had raised their own children. The talk shifted to final plans that would need to be made. "What would you like your obituary to say, Dad?" they asked, and the oldest took notes. "What hymn or scripture would you like in your funeral service?" the middle son asked. His father replied, "How Great Thou Art."

He died a little more than three months later. And as the middle son, though I have many regrets about my relationship with Dad, for this one thing I will always be grateful: that last Christmas, we were together, speaking to one another with love, putting the past hurts behind us, loving one another just as Christ has loved us.

He gave me his blessing that day. The one I longed for so much as a child. The one I desperately want to make sure my sons and daughters do not grow up without.

Thanks, Dad. I love you, too.

Appendix A

Small Groups for Accountability

In *The Journal of Family Ministry*, Vol. 1.2, Ken Canfield's article entitled "The Modern Fatherhood Movement and Ministry to Fathers in the Faith Community," includes the following important paragraphs:

Although there are many ways to engage fathers—to help them to process the effects of fatherlessness, or to develop as fathers—facilitating a small group appears to be one of the most effective. Why? As noted by other researchers, most social behavior occurs in groups. When fathers get together to compare and to discuss issues that arise related to their fathering, learning is enhanced.

Small groups can have a powerful impact on how individuals learn. The notion of "cooperative learning" is richly demonstrated in fatherhood groups. When asked after a group meeting, "What was the most helpful insight a father gained?" fathers reported that the shared experience in lis-

tening to other men was most helpful, particularly when a failure or shortcoming was revealed. The listening also prepared and helped fathers form new ways of thinking and to develop new habits related to their fathering. (p. 31)

My experience would confirm these findings, and I am encouraged by a weekly meeting of an "Iron Man Group." The group size has ranged from two to five men. The purpose of this meeting is to sharpen one another as iron sharpens iron by asking each other questions about our spiritual disciplines, our marriage and family, our leadership, our sexual purity, our financial integrity, and more. There are a number of men in our church who are involved in Iron Man groups and have benefitted from the encouragement they give and receive there.

There is also a monthly men's breakfast at church on the third Sunday morning at 7:30 a.m. Men and young men, ages 12 and up, are invited to come and eat together (a team of men cooks each month), hear a speaker, and fellowship. This is not a "small group," but the social interaction around the tables is rich and helpful.

Finally, we have an annual men's retreat, usually at the beach. Again, men and young men, ages 12 and up are invited. The weekend (Thursday – Saturday) includes sessions of worship, Bible study, prayer, and small group accountability. There are also ample hours of recreation on the beach. We all come away from these times together refreshed and encouraged in our journey to faithful manhood.

Appendix B

Four testimonies of family devotions

I asked a few men in the church who lead their families in regular devotions to write down what they do and how they do it. I offer them to you, with their permission.

Jeremy Troxler Family Devotions

For the Troxler family, devotions began as a work the Lord did in me, the father, while I was serving as a youth leader at a previous church. During my time with the youth, there was a striking theme that was obvious both to me and to the youth pastor: it was apparent that the young people from the church body had either very little or no instruction in the Word at home. Based on our frustration, the youth pastor and I developed a curriculum beginning with the very basics (books of the Bible, major themes, basic Bible doctrine) just to attempt to form a foundational understanding for these young people who had been in church their whole lives (sixteen years for some of them).

Based on that experience, I determined in my heart that no one besides me would be responsible for training up my children (my wife and I had one son at that time). I knew that my son would learn from many people, some much more adept and equipped at preaching and teaching than I, but that those instructions would be supplemental in nature, not primary. My wife was on board totally with all this, and we have discussed periodically how things are progressing and ways in which we can improve.

These intentions have only been encouraged and fortified at Antioch Community Church. I have incorporated many ideas obtained from talks, sermons, and discussions in small groups. We currently have four children (three boys and one girl), and our philosophy for training our children is that training is a deliberate, all-day recognition of opportunities to interject the truth of God's Word into daily events. Therefore, our time together in a formal setting varies between three and five times a week. Every day, however, we discuss the things of the Lord as they come up in music, interaction with one another, etc. For example, I recall one night my second son asking for more vitamins (as the chewable form we gave were much like gummy bears). I took that opportunity to talk with all three boys about the more general principle that often things that are good can be bad if we want them too much. We spoke of idols, sins of gluttony, and touched on stewardship. Our formal teaching time varies as well. We have studied books of the Bible, looked at the miracles of Jesus in the Gospels, gone through Proverbs, and at Christmastime every year go through the *Jesse Tree* devotionals. To end each day, we read a portion of a book. We are currently reading through the *Chronicles of Narnia*. We feel it is good to feed the healthy aspects of their imaginations with a message that we can call upon later, as the type of Christ is portrayed in many situations.

We have found our time in training, as it occurs throughout the day, is a blessing both to our children and to my wife and me, as parents. We learn a great deal and have recognized how edifying it is to our family joy and harmony to be intentional and deliberate in having our minds on the Lord all throughout the day. While far from perfect, we thank the Lord for any successes He has brought to bear in us and our children. What has provided most for the continuation of our family instruction has been a determination of the will, by the grace of God, not to have someone else instruct our children, a unity as husband and wife to make training our children a priority (spending time talking about what our formal studies will be and how things are going in the home), and having a strong group of support in both our home group meeting and in our church body. It is a challenge and encouragement to see so many families focused as we are to train up our children in the way they should go. It is also a great help to hear, often, the necessity and priority it should be in the home.

A word of testimony in closing. We send our children back for Vacation Bible School each summer to the church where we used to attend, as we have friends and family that work the event and request we allow our boys to participate. Each summer we see and hear how our children "pick up" the teaching so quickly and can "teach the lesson after the first night." It is a blessing to be able to respond that our children know the lessons because it's not their first time hearing them. They know the stories in the Bible because they have heard them before many times. This is a testimony to what the Lord can do in a child's heart, not an attempt to boast in personal success, and we use that opportunity to challenge the parents to do the same in their own homes and see the fruit that is born. We are thankful for the experiences in the past that prompted us to take action in our own home in taking up the responsibility to train our children in the fear and admonition of the Lord, the encouragement in the present in seeing our children develop in God's truth, and we look forward to the fruit that will be borne in the future from seeds that are planted today.

David Ball Family Devotions

Consistent family devotions is an area in which I struggled mightily, up until the first shepherds' meeting. I still have the notes I took from that meeting, though not in front of me right now, and when Mark was discussing the qualifications of a shepherd, he mentioned a man who leads "consistent family devotions." When that was said, it pierced my heart because I had not led a consistent family devotion in quite some time. I had gone through "hot" periods, in which I was consistently leading devotions; however, that was the exception and not the norm.

I thought about declaring myself unworthy to be a shepherd and leaving the meeting, and perhaps a more godly man would have, I don't know, but God has used that meeting in a mighty way in the lives of our family.

I tried to do our devotions at night after dinner; then after dinner and an email check; then after dinner, an email check, and an ESPN check. Very quickly it was 9-9:30, and I was tired and not interested in doing the devotion, but in getting the kids to bed. When doing my checklist, I was hoping Susan would "forget" to mention the devotion, and she recently told me that she would hope that I would "forget" to do the devotion. If a devotion was done, many times, in my opinion, it was a dead work. I was not interested in glorifying the Lord, but checking off a chore. I'd hurry through it in ten lifeless minutes, or less, then pray for God's blessing and send the kids off to bed. One night, shortly after the shepherds' meeting, we sat down for our devotions, and I told Susan and the kids how I was feeling. I told them that, even though we might only do two devotions on a "good" week, I could not continue to do devotions in this manner.

We talked and decided to switch our devotion time to the morning, because my mornings are usually very flexible. We would wake up early the next morning to start our devotions at 6:30 a.m. I was surprised that the kids were somewhat excited by this, and they woke up the next morning, ready and eager to go. We had some prayer time, some reading/teaching time, and some more prayer time. When we were finished, I was shocked to see that about an hour had passed! It passed so quickly, and it didn't feel like a chore, or more importantly, a dead work. Christ visited our devotion that morning and breathed life into it. The kids were excited, Susan was excited, and I was excited! I remember one exchange between Garrett and Virginia as they were heading off to bed, expressing the excitement and anticipation of the next morning's devotion: Virginia said, "I'm going to get up early at 5:30!" to which Garrett replied, "Oh yea, well I'm going to set my alarm for 5:27!"

I believe we have missed a couple mornings. Last week I can remember we skipped one morning because we didn't get home from home group until close to eleven, and the kids were done in. But those are now the exceptions instead of the norm. We all look forward to getting together in the morning and learning more about the Lord. We have been going through John MacArthur's devotional "Strength for Today," and we've been reading through Proverbs, and it has been magnificent. Our devotions, once dead, have been made alive by the power of Christ, and to Him be all honor and glory!

Mark Kemp Family Devotions

We do family devotions in the morning from 6:30 to 7:00 a.m. I usually try to have a personal devotion before that. It may be in the form of a reading, Oswald Chambers, a book I am reading, or even prayer. Hope and the kids will join me at the kitchen table, and we will begin our study. I usually have each person read 2-5 verses until we have finished the chapter or portion of a chapter. This has always been Scripture. We have considered a different book, but I prefer the Scriptures. The kids and I have read books together and used other time to go over it. We have gone through Proverbs many times. We have done Old and New Testament books over the years. We meet Monday through Friday. Saturday and Sunday, I encourage everyone to have more time for personal devotion in the morning. There have been times it was difficult to meet due to schedules, sickness, travel, work, and then there is the ongoing battle to keep the group together. One may not want to get up for one reason or another. I made it a rule, if you were late or could not come due to illness, then all other activities that day were also missed (Arts Alive, social events and TV, etc.) On days when I miss due to the Iron Man group I am in, Hope will usually lead the time.

After the reading I have some prepared questions to try to stimulate discussion. It usually does not require much before there is a lot of participation. Hope is always helpful and supportive in that area. We then will transition into prayer requests. I go from person to person, and each must have at least one request; most the time there are numerous ones. We will discuss these briefly so that we can go straight to prayer, which we also do in the circle, with me usually going last. Many times after prayer we will have brief family planning where I may talk with one of the kids about schedules, chores, school, work, or anything pressing. By this time, it is around 7:15 or 7:20, and I need to get to work.

What led me to do family devotions was a combination of things. First was the encouragement from my elders at church and others who were doing them. Second was that it seemed every time I read a good book about fatherhood, leadership, manhood, parenting, loving my wife, it always seemed to come back to the foundation of family devotion time together, regular-consistent-daily-enthusiastic, etc. And third, but probably most important, I saw the need. The need in my kids for their dad to be with them and share teaching/learning, prayer, time, and everything we do together. The need in my wife for me to step up to the plate and lead. She wanted me to be over her and lead her and the children. She wanted me to protect her. She needed a real Man, not one who was leading on the fly, passively and with sporadic interest. She craved the intimacy of spiritual leadership in me. It really was not a hard decision to make once I woke up and smelled the coffee . . . (pun intended).

The keys to consistency have been accountability. I already said that I wake every one up. That may not be the best way, but it works for us. I would rather each person get themselves up. I did not push that requirement. I require each to sit up, have their Bible, participate, and I have found that is what they also want. If I lead they will join right in. The times we have struggled and gotten off schedule or missed mornings is usually due to my lack of leadership, quite honestly. Sometimes they have said it was boring, but then I hear them talking to others about it with positive comments. I do allow some input on what we study which has helped them feel a leadership role, mainly for my sons. Hope has always been open to whatever I want to study. Adjustments were tricky when Becca went to college, when David had morning workouts, when school terms changed, and other times.

God has been faithful. I want to stay obedient.

David Bainbridge Family Devotions

I spent my early childhood without a father. My mom married very young, and my birth father left her when I was about three. Because she had to work to support us, I was raised primarily by her parents, my Grandmother and Grandaddy. They were godly people that loved the Lord, and they raised me in the "fear and admonition" of Him.

I loved my Grandaddy. Although he was the only man I ever heard say the famous phrase, "This is gonna hurt me more than it's gonna hurt you," I knew that he loved me as much as I loved him. He spent as much time with me as he possibly could. Even through high school he was always around, always supporting me in whatever extra-curricular events I did. He was often the first "fan" to arrive and the last to leave. I have many, many, extremely fond memories of my Grandaddy!

Unfortunately, I don't have *any* memories of Grandaddy ever leading us in any kind of devotional or Bible-reading time. I sat next to him in church every Sunday (morning and evening), listening to him belt out all the old hymns in a not-so-great voice. I heard him say the best, most heartfelt blessings at mealtime, complete with "thees" and "thous," but in all my years in his house, I don't recall one time when we sat down and read the Bible, or sang a song of praise, or even said bedtime prayers together. I *knew* he loved the Lord. He modeled a manly Christian life for me, but we *never* talked about it. I've heard the saying plenty of times that "more is caught than taught," but one regret I have from my youth is that Grandaddy never actually told me why he loved Jesus and why I should too.

In fact, Grandmother was always the one who led me in the ways of the Lord. Everyday when I would get up, I would find her in the den on her knees reading the Word and praying. She would welcome me into her arms and read the Psalms to me in such a wholehearted and thoroughly joyful, thankful way that I couldn't help but be attracted to what she was experiencing as a child of God. At the same time, Grandmother ran the house with a rather strict, perfectionist, and something-quite-less-than-submissive attitude. You either did it her way, or you were somewhat less than equal. One thing I've learned as I've matured is that while rules and expectations are absolutely good and necessary as Christian parents, they always need to be balanced with grace.

Now I understand some of the reasons for these dynamics in my grandparents' house. They had been the typical post-World War II family, where the man was a solid, steady provider out in the workplace, and the wife was the safe and stable keeper of the comfortable home. Certain things weren't talked about; you just did what was expected of you, and didn't do what good "Christian" people *don't* do.

While it pains me severely to write anything negative about my Grandaddy that I loved so dearly, I now see that there are important lessons that can be learned from his life, especially as it relates to fatherhood. See, Grandaddy had two sons of his own, in addition to my Mom, and I'm sure they were brought up in a very similar environment as I. They all excelled in academics, athletics, music, and whatever else they were involved in, based on the driving force of my Grandmother. They had an outstanding head-knowledge of the Bible (evidenced by all of their quizzing and speaking awards), but their heart-knowledge was never fostered, especially by their father. For them, it was all about *what* they knew, not *Who* they knew.

The most condemning piece of evidence to me that Grandaddy failed to properly execute his biblical role as husband and father by not daily instructing his wife and children (especially his sons) in the Word of God, and by rarely (if ever) telling them of his love for the Lord, is the result of his children's marriages. All three of their first marriages ended in divorce. They were certainly all adults and responsible for their own decisions, but I can't help but think that with a good bit more biblical instruction from their father (especially on how much God *hates* divorce), things might have turned out for the better within those families. At the same time, I know God is sovereign, and the thought has occurred to me that He also lets us make our own mistakes, perhaps for the sole purpose that those who follow after us in our own families can learn from them.

That's a fairly good segue to my adolescent and teen-age years. While my mom's first marriage ended in di-vorce at the very young age of twenty-two, the Lord pro-vided in countless ways for us for the next six years until she met and married the man I've called Dad since I was nine. Dad had also married young and been divorced, and had two children of his own that lived with their mother in California. But, he was from a respected family in our hometown and home church, and we were delighted to have the stability of a traditional-looking family.

Unfortunately, the "stability" Dad's arrival brought was not quite what we had expected. He had been brought up in a similar environment as Mom, so he did not have a bib-lically-sound fatherly example. Dad's father was a respect-ed local business owner who provided well for his family, was a head usher in the church, and was heavily involved in the Gideons. His mother was a meticulous keeper of the home, as well as a much-loved Sunday School teacher with a constant, loving smile. Again, the letter of the law had been followed, and all appearances were Christian, but *no* father-son discipleship had ever occurred.

Those first few years after Dad's arrival were spent by Mom and him building his small business into a successful enterprise. In fact, I saw even less of Mom during that time than I had when she was working just to support the two of us. We essentially ended up sacrificing any quality family time for the "stability" of two working parents bringing in constant excess cash flow. Honestly though, at the time, I was quite happy. I didn't know that I wasn't being properly equipped for manhood, and more accurately, Christian fatherhood. I enjoyed the independence their absence afforded me. I was free to play with all my friends in the neighborhood until the sun went down, and I pretty much did whatever I wanted, all within the bounds of the expected "good Christian boy."

As the business became more successful, we moved to a bigger house outside the city limits and started accumulating more and more "toys." As happens so often with "self-made" financial successes, Mom and Dad never really slowed down to enjoy the fruits of their labors, but kept working harder and harder to make and accumulate as much as they possibly could. In hindsight, those early teenage years were where I really needed a Christian father's discipleship. It was during those years that I, as well as a majority of unsupervised boys that age, developed bad habits as it relates to how we view the opposite sex. Because Dad had never been around long enough for us to develop a bond or trust, on the few occasions that I can recall him trying to have a conversation with me about girls and/or sex, I just blew him off. I was *never* taught by my dad how to properly respect and treat a woman. He never taught me God's design or the biblical message regarding the roles of men and women.

In fact, I can recall maybe five times when we as a family opened the Bible and/or prayed together, and that was at my mom's direction. She got us each our own copy of *The One Year Bible*, and we sat down to read it together, but that lasted a week at the most. Never before or after do I remember speaking with either of my parents about anything specific in the Bible. I went to a Christian school and was always either at church with the youth group or hanging out with my youth group friends elsewhere, so it was expected that I was learning all that I needed related to Christianity in those environments. And, in reality, I probably was *hearing* all I should have needed to hear from those sources. But, because I didn't have the accountability of a close biblical father-son relationship, I was free to develop poor Bible study and prayer habits, as well as explore sinful desires, without much fear of consequences.

Dad and I never did become very close. I'm sure at some point he tried a little, and I pushed him away, so he gave up. We endured each other through my high school years, but never had any meaningful conversations, discipleship-related or otherwise. As I look back now, being left alone so much and the independence I greatly enjoyed as a result, are probably the primary contributors to a young adult life of struggle against the flesh. I never learned self-denial in any way, be it from food or from sexual desire or anything else I wanted. I never learned and, in fact, completely resisted any transparency or accountability with anyone. This resulted in many complications in my young married life as well. So many confrontations Michelle and I had in our first fifteen years related to money or sex or even just time-management could have been avoided if I'd had a biblical discipling relationship with my Dad.

I've provided all that background to help the reader understand why I feel so strongly about a father's God-given role as the spiritual leader of his house, and why we have emphasized family devotions and discipleship so much in our family. This may sound too harsh, but I can almost say that most of what I have done or tried to do as a father has intentionally been the opposite of what was modeled for me in my immediate and extended families during my childhood and teenage years. One of my primary motivations as a father has been to *not* have that said about me by my children when they become parents.

As I approached fatherhood in the year 2000 and continued to struggle with my own self-discipline, I *knew* that one thing we would always do as a family would be to have some type of family devotions. I'm not sure what convinced me – probably the Holy Spirit now that I think about it – but I was determined that this was one facet of fatherhood in which I was *not* going to fail!

Unfortunately, that determination led to many frustrating nights as our active firstborn son turned into an incredibly stubborn toddler, and subsequently a three-year-old terror, that *would not* sit still and listen! At the time, we didn't have any sort of experience or examples to follow in child training within our church (before we came to Antioch) or extended family, so my idea of discipline was more of the "make them obey by sheer force and anger" method. It still makes me want to cry when I think of all the times I would fight him to "beat his butt" when what he truly needed was firm but patient and loving correction and instruction in the Word – *training*. Obviously, my method only made things worse. It didn't matter how good the Bible stories were or how short I made them; he was so disruptive that I was sure nothing was getting through to him or his little siblings.

As we were pregnant with our fourth child in five years, we began wondering like most modern families if this would be our last. At the same time, our oldest was soon to turn five, and we were beginning to consider what to do about schooling. I believe the Lord providentially led us – my wife first – to many great homeschooling resources that showed us clearly that that was the direction He would have us to take for our children.

In addition, and just as providentially, within the online homeschooling community we had now become a part of, there was an offshoot that the Lord really used to speak to our hearts about the blessing of children and the special gifts that they are from Him. We were now finally beginning to understand how precious they are to Him first, and to us second, as treasures created by Him for us to desire and cherish. Our eyes were opened to the fact that *properly* training and disciplining children, consistently and firmly, but always in love with a healthy amount of grace, was the key to their hearts as well as the clear prescription in God's Word.

Since then, while we have failed countless times, we have always been focused on that primary purpose – *that our job as parents is to treasure each one of the precious children God gives us (however many that might be) and to train them according to His Word, teaching them to love Him with all their heart, with all their mind, and with all their strength, and to love and serve others more than themselves.* The desire we believe the Lord has put in our hearts is to mold a family with a multi-generational faithfulness to His Word and to each other. Families these days, including our extended ones, are so splintered and divided because we've largely departed from the biblical model.

I'll attempt now to outline several "things" we believe in doing, do currently, or have done in aiming toward our primary purpose as stated above. These are in somewhat of a random order.

We always have dinner together as a family around the table every night that we are home. That is of utmost importance to us. The conversation is not always that great or edifying (sometimes it's completely ridiculous), but we are together and we are building memories as a family.

We have for several years read the "Proverb of the day" at breakfast (For example, on October 5th, we would read Proverbs chapter 5, not something Confucius or Joel Osteen once said.). More recently, we've been having our oldest son be the reader as a means of encouraging him in his natural leadership role of his younger siblings, as well as helping them see him and respect him in that role. We will likely begin alternating him with our second son in the near future.

In the past when our oldest three were old enough, but the younger ones were not, the three oldest would each have a night of the week where they would get to stay up later than everyone else for some one-on-one time with Daddy, playing games or reading books or something like that. Once the younger ones got a little older, it just became impractical and left too little time for my wife and me. More recently, we have been alternating weeks taking one of the older three out to breakfast with Daddy as a time of discipleship. I've been assigning them something to do in between our breakfasts, and they are to journal their success or lack thereof and bring that journal with them to our next breakfast. I'm sure this will evolve as we continue, and more of the children get old enough to join me. The purpose is intentional one-on-one discipleship as well as just plain fellowship and bonding, which we feel like we have not had enough of in the past.

We have devotions and prayer right before bedtime at least five nights a week. We have tried doing mornings on several occasions, but it has never worked out for us. Not sure if we'll ever be able to get there, but it's a goal. We have done many different things for devotions in the past. While I said earlier that I committed to *not failing* in this area, our desire has also been to not be ritualistic or militant about it, but to demonstrate the need for consistent and fruitful time in the Word of God, together and individually.

When all we had was little ones and "pre-readers," we would read their little "My First Bibles" with all the pictures and cartoon drawings.

When our oldest three got old enough, we started incorporating skits on occasion, where they would act out some of the great stories in the Bible.

We've done some singing, although that's one thing I would like to do more of. My goal is to learn to play my guitar so I can facilitate this better. My children may beat me to it at this rate, though, because they are already getting very good at piano. I'm sure that will soon turn into guitar for at least one of them.

We went through a season, when we had one of my wife's teenage cousins living with us, that we just started reading through certain books of the New Testament, as much for her education as for our children's. What a *joy* when the Lord took all that she had learned as a temporary part of our family and church, and used it to speak to her heart and *save her soul*! I'll never forget that! It was sometimes hard to stick with, because the words of the Bible don't always make sense right away to young children. But we did stick with it because we knew that she had never really heard or understood the simple truths of the love and grace of God demonstrated through the gift of His Son Jesus Christ.

There was a two-year period – and that may have been when Michelle's cousin lived with us – that my wife and kids read through the whole Bible as part of their home-schooling schedule. That was a significant accomplishment we celebrated with a special dinner to help them understand how valuable God's Word is, and how necessary it is for us to be committed to reading and learning it.

We've been through a couple of Christian character-building books, one by Clay Clarkson called *Our 24 Family Ways*, which we went through twice. This one especially was packed with Scripture and was very beneficial to us all. Each "family way" was discussed for an entire week, with a new Scripture passage for each day of that week, so it was good for at least half a year of study.

We have currently scaled back a little bit on what we are doing for devotions for several reasons. Right now, we are reading one or two stories a night from a series of old illustrated Bible story books written by Arthur Maxwell (also known as Uncle Arthur). My primary reason for this is that we have several younger children who are still learning the basics of the Bible that the older ones have known for awhile, so I think they benefit from hearing the stories told a little more simply with illustrations. I understand the argument that the Word of God is sufficient to speak to all, no matter the age or education level, but I also believe it makes sense to make it more "understandable" to little ones, as long as I'm there to elaborate or clear up any confusion that they might have.

We have always put a significant emphasis on memorizing Scripture, and have often rehearsed during our devotion time. Back when we had just three kids, and our youngest was able to talk, we set to memorizing Psalm 23, Psalm 100, Philippians 4:4-8, and other important yet relatively simple passages.

CPSIA information can be obtained at www.ICGtesting.com
Printed in the USA
LVOW080142020713

341063LV00001B/5/P